Yes, You Can!

Overcome Crises with God's Help

AN INTERACTIVE DEVOTIONAL JOURNAL FOR WOMEN

PRAISE FOR YES, YOU CAN!

If you're looking for a challenging devotional offering help with relationships, this book will meet that need. Beth and Jeanette have combined their writing skills to present a heartfelt work filled with personal experiences and encouragement from God's Word. If you desire to increase the strength of your relationships with not only family and friends but with God, as well, *Yes, You Can!* is the book for you.

—Marsha Hubler, best-selling author and director of the Montrose Christian Writers Conference

Reading the writing of Beth Gormong and Jeanette Levellie is like sharing a cup of coffee on the back porch with some old friends. The writing style is engaging, inspiring, and uplifting. Their sincerity and deep faith come through every word. I especially enjoy the questions and suggestions for engaging my heart with the Lord at the end of each entry. I am all about practicing my faith in tangible ways. The questions, journaling, and prayer prompts allow me to tangibly lean into the Holy Spirit and discover what he might be saying to me.

—Pastor Gary Thomas, Paris Assembly of God Church, author, and artist

Yes, You Can! offers hope to the discouraged and weary through personal experiences as a springboard to the miracles, truth, and answers found when we focus on God instead of the lies one tends to believe. *Yes, You Can!* gives witness of God's constant presence, from the childless bearing a child to overcoming fear. Instead of focusing on the stressor, *Yes, You Can!* encourages you to focus on *the* Overcomer, Jesus! Instead of saying "I can't," you will shout, "Yes, I Can!"

—Lisa M Buske, speaker, host—*Keeping it Real* podcasts, author, *Where's Heidi? One Sister's Journey*

Jeremiah 29:11 says, "For I know the plans I have for you," declares the Lord, "plans to give you hope and a future." Beth Gormong and Jeanette Levellie's new book *Yes, You Can!* shares encouraging examples of how trusting in God provides boundless opportunities and assurance of hope in the process.

—Susan Hayhurst, freelance writer and columnist

What I like best about Beth Gormong and Jeanette Levellie's new book, *Yes, You Can!* is the practical, Scripture-based help for real-life situations. It's like sitting beside a good friend who encourages you (and almost as cozy as snuggling up with a golden retriever!).

—Peggy Frezon, contributing editor, *All Creatures* magazine, author, *The Dog in the Dentist Chair*

Beth Gormong and Jeanette Levellie (known for her humorous and heartfelt essays) turn to heavier topics while retaining their warmth and wisdom on every honest and encouraging page. You will be convinced that *Yes, You Can!*

—James Watkins, author and speaker

I've known Beth and Jen for many years and have seen God at work in their lives in miraculous ways. The stories in *Yes, You Can!* will give women courage and hope for their own miracles.

—**Diane Stark**, author and conference speaker

Yes, You Can!

Overcome Crises with God's Help

AN INTERACTIVE DEVOTIONAL JOURNAL FOR WOMEN

BETH GORMONG & JEANETTE LEVELLIE
Coloring Pages by Beth Gormong

PUBLISHING THE POSITIVE

ELK LAKE PUBLISHING INC
Plymouth, Massachusetts

Cover and Interior Design: Derinda Babcock

Editor(s): Judy Hagey, Deb Haggerty

PUBLISHED BY: Elk Lake Publishing, Inc., 35 Dogwood Drive, Plymouth, MA 02360, 2020

Library Cataloging Data

Names: Gormong, Beth and Levellie, Jeanette (Beth Gormong and Jeanette Levellie)

Yes, You Can!—Overcome Crises with God's Help / Beth Gormong and Jeanette Levellie

196 p. 23cm × 15cm (9in × 6 in.)

Identifiers: ISBN-13: 978-1-64949-055-1 (paperback) | 978-1-64949-056-8 (trade paperback) | 978-1-64949-057-5 (e-book)

Key Words: Christian Living, Intimacy with God, Prayer, Mercy, Grace, Redemption, Friendship

LCCN: 2020944355 Fiction

DEDICATION

To my God, who promised me he would never leave me or forsake me, and to my "sisters" who blessed me with their beautiful stories. I am rich because you are in my life.
—Beth

To my loving heavenly Father, the God of Yes! and to my dear friend Diana Savage, who has overcome countless impossibilities and has shown me how to find gold in every mud puddle. Thank you!
—Jeanette

CONTENTS

ACKNOWLEDGMENTS

Thank you:

- To my God, the God who helps us overcome the impossibilities in our lives.
- To my husband, Jeff, the real cook and "dough" maker in the family. Thank you for feeding me and paying all the bills so I can write.
- To my Jaena, Jessica, Barb, Marlene, Felicia, Teresa, Jen, and Susan, whose lives have taught me how to persevere and overcome.
- To my coauthor, Jeanette, because she is the reason we make a great team! I'm so thankful you pushed, pulled, encouraged, motivated, and mentored me. Your friendship is one of my greatest treasures.
- To our publisher, Deb Haggerty, for taking a chance on me as an unknown writer.
- To our editors, Diana Savage and Judy Hagey, thank you for finding mistakes we missed. You make us better.
- And finally to my parents, Ernest and Ada, the greatest overcomers I know. Someday I will share your story.

—Beth

- Thank you to my heavenly Father, who is wise enough not to allow me to manage my own life and is kind enough to say yes when I need to hear it.

- To my husband, Kevin, who has been on this marriage-go-round with me for four and a half decades. You get the biggest trophy!
- To my coauthor, Beth—I am proud of you and so is Jesus. Applause, thanks, and strong coffee.
- To our publisher, Deb Haggerty, and editors, Diana Savage and Judy Hagey, thanks for making our words sparkle. You are life-changers.
- And to our readers, who make us jump for joy. You are worth it.

—Jen

CHAPTER 1

YES, YOU CAN!

Blessed is the one who perseveres under trial because,
having stood the test, that person will receive the crown
of life that the Lord has promised to those who love him.
(James 1:12)

"I can't do it. I can't climb anymore." My thirteen-year-
old daughter sat on a rock and refused to move. Honestly,
I was as tired as she was and grateful for the moment of
rest. But we couldn't quit now, not when we were so close
to the top of this mountain. Flattop was a hill compared to
the great Denali off in the distance. But for girls from the
flatlands of Indiana, it was a mountain, nevertheless.

Earlier that day as we started the climb, I began to worry.
*What am I doing here? I'm so out of shape. I'm thirty-nine,
too old for climbing mountains for Pete's sake.* But I kept my
thoughts to myself and tried to maintain the same pace as
the others.

The climb was beautiful. We paused several times to take
in the views. My sister-in-law's thoughtfulness had as much
to do with the breaks as the actual scenery. Marlene realized
I was struggling. My legs ached after the first hour, just when
the climb became more challenging. The steeper we went,
the more slowly my body moved.

Nearly at the top, we were stopped again—not by my weakness this time, but by my daughter's exhaustion. I was shocked. She had seemed so strong and capable and hadn't complained at all. Now, I realized we had both kept our true thoughts about the climb to ourselves, and both of us ended up struggling.

But we had to go on. We would be disappointed in ourselves if we stopped anywhere but at the top. So we sat for a few minutes, catching our breath and passing around water bottles. Then Marlene took Jaena's arm, helped her up, and led her the rest of the way. "You can do this, Beth," I heard God whisper. "Both of you can do this."

Sitting at the summit of Flattop was one of the greatest emotions in the world. We'd made it! We'd done it! We climbed a mountain! The air was refreshing, the view spectacular from every direction.

None of us wanted to head back down. We could have stayed on the summit for hours, basking in our accomplishment. But rainclouds in the distance informed us now was the time to descend. Soon we were heading into the hardest part of the trip for me. Going down, I could see how high we were, and the view activated my fear of heights. As I looked at the world below, everything in my body said, "No! Stand still. Unsafe!" But my mind said, "You can't stay up here forever. You have to move."

As I clung to the side of the mountain, I learned to lean into the Rock—Christ Jesus. Panic threatened to overtake me, but I couldn't let it stop me. I had to move one foot in front of the other, one tiny step at a time, all the way down the steep mountainside. Just as we reached the bottom, the rain began, and we bolted for the car.

The next day, my head and body ached. "I'll never be able to move again." I moaned and rolled gingerly onto my side. It took all my strength to get out of bed. Slowly, during a period of awkward, achy movements, my body recovered.

We all face mountains in our lives. For some of us, the hardest part is the beginning. For others, the difficulty comes on the way up, and we want to quit. For others still, it's the walk down the opposite side. Heights intimidate us. And then there's the recovery time afterward when our bodies complain.

Maybe you've experienced difficult climbs in your life. Maybe you're in the middle of one now. Or maybe you're looking at a hard situation, wishing you could just turn around and avoid all the pain you sense is ahead.

When we stand at the bottom of a mountain, the challenge seems impossible. Sometimes we can't see a path. But we can believe that God is always with us. The Bible says, "Be strong and courageous. Do not be afraid or terrified because of them, for the Lord your God goes with you; he will never leave you nor forsake you" (Deuteronomy 31:6).

God shows up in different ways. Perhaps it's through encouragement from a friend who walks with us, supporting and helping us take the next steps. Sometimes we sense his power when we need supernatural strength or wisdom. At other moments, he fills us with the courage we need to get up and move on. Often times, his help comes after we have prayed for many hours. But he is with us every moment— at the beginning of the climb, during our weakest middle moments, and at the top of the mountain.

He is always with us. Always.

—Beth

"Only those who will risk going too far can possibly find out how far they can go."—T.S. Eliot

PROMPT:

Write about a time when you observed God's presence in a difficult situation.

_____

_____

_____

_____

_____

_____

_____

_____

_____

Pray this prayer with me. "Lord, thank you for your constant presence. Help me see how you lead me, give me courage, and strengthen me. I trust in you in the impossible situation I face today."

Amen.

CHAPTER 2

PRAY FOR ME

Stand firm, and you will win life. (Luke 21:19)

"Hurry! Take him some clean clothes." Esther thrust some freshly laundered robes at the servant. Outside the palace walls, her Uncle Mordecai was running around in sackcloth with ashes on his head. *What a scene.* But just a few minutes later, the servant was back, clothes in his hands.

"He won't accept them."

"Go. Find out why he is acting this way." Esther waved the servant away in frustration. *What could be going on in his mind? Why is he so distraught?*

Her uncle informed her that her new husband, the king, had issued a decree that would put all her relatives to death.

"None of us will be safe if the king's decree is carried out," Mordecai warned. "It says all Jews must be killed. *All* Jews, Esther. You are the only one in a position to save us. If you plead with the king, it's possible he will change his mind. Who knows? Maybe you were chosen queen for this very reason."

Mordecai's words echoed through her head. *What can I do? I can go before the king only if invited. It's been thirty days since he's called for me. It's possible he won't even allow me to see him once I ask. And if I'm allowed into his presence, I'll have to tell him I'm a Jew—the secret I've tried so hard to keep hidden.*

Esther lay on her bed, staring at the elaborate painting covering the ceiling. Soon this luxurious lifestyle with its lotions, perfumes, and fancy clothing might end. The queen's life—her life—was in danger from the man who had just chosen her for his wife. That was an unimaginable thought for someone living a pampered life in a palace. Esther fought the urge to run back to the safe arms of her uncle like she'd done as a child. But that wouldn't solve anything. Now was the time for her to be the strong one.

Esther understood her only hope would come from God. She had sent Mordecai a request—to pray and to tell all the other Jews to pray. She needed the Lord's protection and a plan if she was to go before the king.

"Lord, help me," she prayed. Tears soaked her pillow as she lay begging God to answer.

By morning she had a plan, and God gave her favor with the king, who granted her the audience she needed, not once, but twice. At the end of those two meetings, Esther presented her dilemma to him. He immediately issued a decree that saved the entire Jewish population.

When we find ourselves in impossible situations, prayer should be our first step. Unfortunately, many times I find myself panic-stricken on my bed before I remember to cry out to God. But as children of the all-powerful, all-seeing God, we can trust confidently in his ability to answer our needs. Our God is a big-picture God. We can trust in God's vision.

—Beth

"I am not afraid... I have God... It was for this that I was born."—Joan of Arc

Prompt:

Think about a problem you are facing right now. Write out a prayer to God. Express your pain, fears, confusion. Ask him for the answer you need. Ask him to show you the big picture.

_____

_____

_____

_____

_____

_____

_____

_____

_____

Read the book of Esther to see the biblical account of this remarkable woman.

CHAPTER 3

GOD'S LITTLE SURPRISE

"'If you can'?" said Jesus. "Everything is possible for one who believes." (Mark 9:23)

"How is Francie?" I asked my friend, Carla, when we met at Christmastime. Carla's daughter, Francie, had been trying to conceive for the last eight years, and she and her husband, Brad, had seen numerous doctors and suffered through grueling tests. But the couple was still childless.

"Physically, she's fine," said Carla. "Just discouraged. She and Brad recently celebrated their tenth anniversary. I think she's afraid she'll soon get too old to conceive."

"I'll pray for her," I said, which sounded trite. I knew Carla and lots of others must be praying for Francie to conceive. What difference would my prayers make? Still, I kept my word, asking God to give Brad and Francie a child.

A while later, as I read Psalm 113, I noticed verse 9: "He settles the childless woman in her home as a happy mother of children." *Wow, I never saw that verse before.* With my favorite purple pen, I wrote Francie's name and the date next to the verse. Before I'd finished writing, a strong voice resonated in my heart: "Francie will have a baby a year from now."

The next time I saw Carla, I told her about the Bible verse and the voice. She stared at me for a few seconds, raised her eyebrows, and said, "We shall see."

On Valentine's Day, Carla called me. "Francie and Brad signed up with an adoption agency," she said. "They may have to wait a few years to get a baby. But at least they've started the process." I was happy the young couple wouldn't have to go through any more painful medical procedures. But I questioned God. *I thought that was your voice I heard back in December. Was I making it up because I want Francie to be a mom?*

Through the spring, summer, and autumn months I continued to pray for Francie and Brad, reminding God of his promise to give barren women children. But by Christmas, my faith started to sag. Carla and I arranged our usual Christmas get-together at a local café. Would she mention my prediction of ten months earlier and laugh it off? Or would she choose not to bring it up for fear I'd be embarrassed that it hadn't come true?

When Carla sat at our corner table, her smiling face glowed. "The adoption agency connected Francie and Brad with a pregnant lady who wants to give up her baby. She's due in April. I'm gonna be a grandma!" I congratulated my dear friend. *Is this what you meant, Lord?* I silently asked. I'd been so sure Francie and Brad would have their own child. Maybe the message I'd received meant this adopted baby.

The next few months flew by. I hardly noticed when Valentine's Day came and went—the day I had been so sure Francie would've welcomed her baby. When Carla called on April first to tell me that Brad and Francie had brought their adopted baby girl home, I rejoiced.

A few weeks later—Francie's first Mother's Day—I visited her church. I waited in a long line of well-wishers to see baby Emma. Francie glowed as only a new mama can. Then she handed the baby to Brad and pulled me off to one side. "Guess what!" she whispered in my ear. "We're pregnant!"

My heart nearly burst with joy. "When are you due?" I asked.

"Around Christmas," Francie said, her face alight with joy.

"Then that means …"

"My babies will be eight months apart—can you believe it?"

I nodded, my eyes brimming with happy tears, a sudden light flashing in my brain. Of course. God counts a child from the time of conception. Francie had her baby on Valentine's Day after all—inside her womb. I laughed and said, "Yes, I believe it. That's God for you!"

—Jeanette

"You cannot expect miracles to happen overnight. Be patient, be loving, and little by little, the change you seek will come."—Leon Brown

PROMPT:

Have you ever heard what you thought was God's voice?

_____

_____

_____

_____

_____

_____

_____

_____

If so, and if what he told you hasn't happened yet, don't give up. If that voice was really his, the promise will come to pass. Keep believing for your miracle.

CHAPTER 4

DESPERATE PRAYERS

Do not be anxious about anything, but in every situation,
by prayer and petition, with thanksgiving, present your
requests to God. (Philippians 4:6)

Hannah longed for a child. Her heart ached. Her body
yearned. But year after year, her arms remained empty.

"Why are you crying? Why won't you eat? Isn't my love
worth more than a baby?" her husband asked. Men can be
insensitive. Yet how are they to understand the longings
within a woman's body? So she ate.

The next time they went to the tabernacle to worship,
she began to pray at the altar. As tears rained down her face,
dripping onto the ground, she prayed silently and promised
God: *Please, Lord, look at my distress and hear my cries. See me,
Lord, and give me a son. I will dedicate him to you and give him
back to you. My baby will be your child.*

She prayed so long and so hard, the priest noticed. With
scorn he asked, "What is wrong with you, woman?"

"I am troubled, sir, and full of grief. I was pouring out
my heart to God." She told the priest about her sorrows and
dreams.

The priest's eyes softened, and his voice calmed. "Peace be
with you. May God give you what you long for."

Hannah thanked the priest and walked away a different woman. No longer sad, she had the peace and confidence of one who has been seen and heard.

Nine months later, she held her baby boy and announced, "His name is Samuel because I asked and God gave."

Her love for her son knew no bounds. Because of God's goodness and her previous promise, she dedicated her precious boy to God. God used him in mighty ways. While he was still a small boy, God spoke to him verbally, giving him a warning for Eli, the priest. When it came time to select the first two kings of Israel, Saul and David, God led Samuel to anoint them to reign. Hannah's son was an advisor to the kings of Israel!

First Samuel 2:1–10 says:

Then Hannah said:

"My heart rejoices in the Lord; in the Lord my horn is lifted high. My mouth boasts over my enemies, for I delight in your deliverance.

"There is no one holy like the Lord; there is no one besides you; there is no Rock like our God.

"Do not keep talking so proudly or let your mouth speak such arrogance, for the Lord is a God who knows, and by him deeds are weighed.

"The bows of the warriors are broken, but those who stumbled are armed with strength. Those who were full hire themselves out for food, but those who were hungry are hungry no more. She who was barren has borne seven children, but she who has had many sons pines away.

"The Lord brings death and makes alive; he brings down to the grave and raises up. The Lord sends poverty and wealth; he humbles and he exalts. He raises the poor from the dust and lifts the needy from the ash heap; he seats them with princes and has them inherit a throne of honor.

"For the foundations of the earth are the Lord's; on them he has set the world. He will guard the feet of his faithful servants, but the wicked will be silenced in the place of darkness.

"It is not by strength that one prevails; those who oppose the Lord will be broken. The Most High will thunder from heaven; the Lord will judge the ends of the earth.

"He will give strength to his king and exalt the horn of his anointed."

God discerned Hannah's heart, and he sees ours too. He hears our prayers and answers according to his will. He rewards righteous hearts and our willingness to give to him what is most precious to us.
—Beth

"The significance of a man is not in what he attains, but rather what he longs to attain."—Khalil Gibran

YES, YOU CAN!

PROMPT:

Pray Hannah's prayer.

My heart rejoices in the Lord; in the Lord my horn is lifted high. My mouth boasts over my enemies, for I delight in your deliverance.

There is no one holy like the Lord; there is no one besides you; there is no Rock like our God.

Ask God to help you give him your greatest desires to use for his good.

Read chapters 1 and 2 of 1 Samuel for the biblical account of Hannah.

CHAPTER 5

TURNING "I CAN'T" INTO "I CAN"

For the Spirit God gave us does not make us timid, but gives us power, love and self-discipline. (2 Timothy 1:7)

Why did you study music? You're not good enough.

You want to get a job in camp ministry? You can't make a living.

God called you to vocational ministry? Really! You don't want to work in a church. Just stay here and get a part-time job.

These lies ran through Jaena's mind, working their hardest to confuse and discourage her. She looked at the inspirational tattoo on her wrist with two words: "I can't." The "I" had a line through it, turning it into a cross. The apostrophe was the image of a red drop of blood, a reminder that maybe *she* couldn't, but God could.

A memory from her freshman year returned. She had sat in her dorm room writing the sentence, "I can't," over and over until she filled an entire sheet of paper. She had wrestled with that lie for years. *I'm so tired of telling myself, "I can't."* So, over and over, one sentence at a time, she crossed the words out. She grabbed a push pin and stuck the paper to the bulletin board above her desk, a reminder to remove "I can't" from her vocabulary. A year later, she visited a church friend, a tattoo artist, and had the reminder permanently etched on her wrist.

After college graduation, she got a call from a church in South Dakota, inviting her to a job interview. Because she *really* wanted that job, she boarded a plane and flew to a state she had never visited, where she knew no one. During her flight, Jaena traced the words on her wrist, amazed at the peace she experienced during what should have been a frightening experience. Here she was, a young woman with no experience, applying for a job at a huge church. But the moment she stepped foot in the church building, she sensed she had come home.

A few weeks later, she loaded all her belongings into a U-Haul truck and drove through a blizzard to her new home, where she would be one of four women on the large staff working at the church.

At first, all the sports talk at staff meetings was odd for her. How would she relate to these men? But soon she found her place in the group—her voice in the conversation. Her perspective was heard and valued. She discovered she was needed, not because she was like everyone else, but because she was different.

Jaena now acknowledges the truth. She is good enough, a valuable asset, and a competent employee. She ministers to females in ways no male can. She has a shared experience that deepens relationships, an empathy that helps heal wounds, and a passion that makes her church's ministry better.

Sometimes she still struggles to remember she has a voice worth hearing and a perspective worth seeing. Satan still lies to her, "You can't." But one look at her wrist reminds her of God's truth that "can't" is a lie.

I am a proud mom.

—Beth

"I want to be all that I am capable of becoming."—
Katherine Mansfield

Prompt:

Is it hard to recognize the lies you've listened to? Write
out all the lies you struggle with. Ask God to show you the
truth and to reveal how he wants to use you.

_____

_____

_____

_____

_____

_____

_____

_____

_____

With God's help... Yes, you can!

With God's help... Yes, you can!

With God's help... Yes you can!

With God's help... Yes, you can!

CHAPTER 6

A WOMAN LED THEM

Lead me, Lord, in your righteousness because of my enemies—make your way straight before me. (Psalm 5:8)

A female leader? A woman advising and judging Israel? Unheard of in that culture, but true. Deborah sat and listened to the disagreements brought to her daily. She led well because God gave her wise counsel and judgment.

On a cloudless day, Deborah sent for Barak, the army commander. "This is what the Lord has told me. Take ten thousand men from the tribes of Naphtali and Zebulun and lead them to Mount Tabor. I will lead Sisera, the commander of our enemy's army, to the river and give his entire army into your hands." Deborah said the words with authority because they were a command from God.

"I'll go," said Barak, "but only if you go with me."

Barak's words saddened her. *Is he scared, or does he not trust that what I say is from God?* She wasn't sure, but his answer stung. "Because you didn't do as Jehovah asked," she replied, "a woman will receive the glory in this battle by being the one to kill Sisera."

That was how Deborah found herself marching out to war alongside ten thousand men. They climbed Mount Tabor's rocky slope and looked down onto the blue waters of the Kishon River where Sisera and his army waited. Deborah never could have imagined she would be going into battle. No doubt her stomach was in knots, even though she realized God had promised victory.

The bloody and fierce fighting began, but soon the Israelites began to overtake Sisera and his men. Deborah and Israel's fighters chased them all the way to Kedesh where Sisera was killed by a woman, Jael.

After that battle, Israel enjoyed forty years of peace while Deborah served as judge. The Old Testament records all the leaders, judges, and kings of Israel. Deborah is the only woman listed. Not only did God give her the unusual role of leading the nation as a woman, but he also gave her strength to guide her people, wisdom to settle disputes, and courage to go into battle alongside trained warriors.

Are you a woman in leadership? If so, you realize you need God's help to do well. Being Israel's leader was a difficult job, but God enabled Deborah to do the work she was meant to do. He will equip you too. Trust in him. Turn to him. Listen for his voice.

—Beth

"Every adversity has the seed of an equivalent or greater benefit."—Napoleon Hill

PROMPT:

List the names of those you lead. Beside each person or group, write a prayer asking God for wisdom to discern what they need and how to lead them well. Write down any insights God gives you.

_____

_____

_____

_____

_____

_____

_____

Read chapters 4 and 5 of Judges for the biblical account of Deborah.

CHAPTER 7

JUST IN TIME

I will remember the deeds of the Lord; yes, I will remember your miracles of long ago. I will consider all your works and meditate on all your mighty deeds. (Psalm 77:11–12)

Fear clouded the deep brown eyes of our fourteen-year-old son, Ron. "Are we gonna end up homeless, Mom?"

When our mobile home had sold a month earlier, we thought we had plenty of time to find a new place, pack up all our junk and move. But a few days later, our loan officer called, saying escrow would close in two weeks. Finding a house at a reasonable price in that short time span—in Los Angeles—would require a miracle. A big one.

I smiled, as much to reassure myself as to encourage Ron. "No, son, you don't need to worry about where to live. At the very worst, the Gettys have agreed to let us sleep on their living room floor till we find a house." I sent up a desperate prayer we wouldn't need to resort to that.

Two weeks earlier we'd looked at a townhouse we liked in a good neighborhood. Before signing the contract, we took one final walkthrough and noticed the white carpet the owners had installed throughout the house since our earlier visit. We politely told them we'd changed our minds and trudged to the car.

I gulped. What could I say to Ron to help him overcome his fear? I had no tangible evidence we'd find an affordable home in fourteen days. We had only God's word to take care of us, and my faith in that word. Was it enough?

Looking Ron in the eye, I said, "Dad and I have been married for twenty years. In that time, we've seen God help us through some pretty horrible situations." I began to list all the ways the Lord had delivered us from two decades' worth of impossibilities:

- When the birth of Ron's sister Esther, required a cesarean section, we had no money to pay for it. Our insurance refused to cover the bill, and four thousand dollars might as well have been four million to us in those days. Someone gave us a gift of a hundred dollars. Apart from that, the Lord just provided little by little, till it was all paid off. "I can't explain it, son. If I could, it wouldn't be a miracle."

- Several years later, Kevin was asked to leave his position as youth pastor due to a deacon mismanaging church funds and a resulting shortfall. The elders gave Kevin only thirty days' notice. In our denomination, finding a new ministry takes much longer than one month— sometimes a year or more. But God showed up again. We were hired at a different church within the month, and the board paid Kev for his first week in advance. We didn't even miss a paycheck.

- After we'd purchased a lemon of a vehicle that spent more time at the mechanic's shop than on the road, we were drowning in debt. One night during a break between songs at a gospel concert our family gave at a nearby church, Kevin mentioned our car troubles. He didn't ask for money, just prayer. The next day, the pastor of the church called, asking us to come and pick up a check for from an anonymous person. I couldn't decide whether to faint or shout "hallelujah!" when I looked at the amount: $3,000—enough to pay off our entire debt. I decided on the "hallelujah" option and sang praises all the way home.

Many of our miracles involved financial needs, but others concerned tangled relationships or a need for physical healing. Our loving Father was involved in every area of our lives, leaving nothing untouched by his hand of grace.

My goal was to encourage Ron's faith. But while I rehearsed God's miracles, my own faith grew. I began to stand up on the inside. *God did it before; he will do it again* echoed through my heart.

A few days after my conversation with Ron, a lady stopped by the bookstore where I worked. "Someone told me you're looking for a house to rent," she said. Their home fit our needs beautifully and was located only three miles from my workplace. We moved in just days before escrow closed on our mobile home. God had provided for us once again, proving he never runs out of ways to show how much he cares for his own.

Since the Lord doesn't have favorite kids, you can expect him to come through for you too in miraculous ways. Starting today, spend some time rehearsing his miracles and watch your faith increase.

—Jeanette

"True happiness is to enjoy the present, without anxious dependence upon the future."—Seneca

YES, YOU CAN!

PROMPT:

Are you facing an ocean-size impossibility?

In the lines below, list some ways God has come through for you in the past

_____

_____

_____

_____

_____

_____

_____

List some of God's miracles from your past.

_____

_____

_____

_____

_____

_____

CHAPTER 8

BOWLS OF MERCY

Now to him who is able to do immeasurably more than all we ask or imagine, according to his power that is at work within us, to him be glory in the church and in Christ Jesus throughout all generations, for ever and ever! Amen. (Ephesians 3:20–21)

This is it, the last of our food. What will I feed my son tomorrow? Oh, how I miss my husband! I need his strength and encouragement right now. As a widow, how am I supposed to survive? How can I take care of my son in this famine? The woman bent to gather a few sticks for a fire. Now out of food, she planned to mix her last meager bit of flour and olive oil into bread and bake one final loaf.

Finding more food seemed impossible. As the sun beat down, a headache began to form around her squinting eyes. The temperature was sweltering, just like yesterday and the day before and the day before that. With the ground too hot and dry for grain to grow, there had been no wheat harvest, so everyone was hungry.

A shadow blocked the sunlight, and she looked up to see the form of a man standing over her.

"Woman, would you give me a little water from your jar and a piece of bread?" The prophet Elijah looked as thirsty and hungry as she was.

"Sir, here is some water from the well; but I don't have any bread. At my home, all I have is a tiny bit of flour and olive oil. I'm gathering these sticks for a fire, so I can make a last little meal for my son and me before we die of hunger." The widow handed him the water jug.

"Don't be afraid. Provide for me and see the miracle God will do for you. You will not run out of flour or oil until the rains come again."

"How can this possibly be, sir?" She shook her head, then looked back at the prophet. "But I recognize your reputation as a man of God and will trust that God will provide." Together she and Elijah gathered firewood. When they reached her home, the widow fixed the loaf of bread for their supper.

Just like Elijah promised, from that point on the widow and her son mysteriously had enough flour and oil for that day's bread. The supply never ran dry. Before each meal, she thanked God for his provision.

Like the widow, we experience moments in our lives when we've lost hope. Our problems seem unanswerable. We can't see a way out of our impossible situation. But God sees the future. He has the answers we need. He sees our needs, hears our cries, and understands our pain. He is here for us.

—Beth

"Faith does not operate in the realm of the possible. There is no glory for God in that which is humanly possible. Faith begins where man's power ends."—George Muller

Prompt:

Make a list of your needs. Ask God to show you a solution. Ask him to help you trust him with those needs. When God gives you an answer, go back to your list and write in the solution and the date, creating a log of God's faithfulness. Trust that he will meet your future needs in the same way.

_____

_____

_____

_____

_____

_____

_____

Read 1 Kings 17:7–24 for the biblical account of the widow at Zarephath and Elijah.

CHAPTER 9

RISING ABOVE

I can do all this through him who gives me strength. (Philippians 4:13)

Jessica practically ran out of her advisor's office. She grabbed her phone and pressed speed dial. "Mom. My advisor … he thinks I'm smart! Can you believe it? He said he'd been looking at my record and was impressed with my grades, especially my statistics grade. He even told me—and he said he doesn't tell very many people this—but he thought I could handle it. There's a way I could skip past working on a master's degree and go straight to a getting a doctorate. Mom, I can't breathe."

She'd said the whole thing in one quick breath, and I could understand why she was excited.

"He asked me where I learned to have such drive," she continued. "I told him about my dyslexia and how I've learned to work twice as hard as others so that they won't see my difficulties. He ended by saying, 'Wouldn't it be great to be called Dr. Jessica Gormong?' Can you believe that, Mom?"

A few months later, Jessica and I sat at the kitchen table reminiscing about that conversation, a monumental moment in a very difficult educational journey. We remembered the many painful moments when Jessica had struggled to learn to read.

"Mom," she'd said, "the lines move. The letters get all scrambled up. My eyes hurt. I hate reading. I'm so dumb."

As those words echoed in our memories, Jessica began to share something I had not heard before. "One day in elementary school, my reading teacher was gone during my normal time with her. I had to leave for lunch with the rest of my regular class. All the others were required to spell a word correctly before leaving for the cafeteria. I was worried because I didn't normally have spelling words. When the teacher got to me, she asked me to spell 'house.' Mom, I didn't know how to spell it. I sat there all panicky. Then I spelled, 'h-o-m-e.' 'Close enough,' she said, smiling and waving me on to lunch."

I smiled too at Jessica's ingenuity. She was always a quick thinker, just not a fast reader. I stole a spoonful of the untouched ice cream sitting in front of Jessica as she launched into a story about eighth grade. Things changed for her when Mrs. Bennett became her English teacher.

"Mrs. Bennett cared about me. She always gave me big hugs at church. Without her, I wouldn't be able to read. Remember that year, Mom? They made a special award for me for the highest reading level improvement in one year in the entire school, third grade to eighth grade."

Gratitude filled my heart at the compassion of that one special teacher.

"Mom," Jessica continued, "through working twice as hard as others, I learned to love learning." She smiled, realizing her perseverance had made all the difference.

Sometimes we face situations we cannot control. Those moments can appear overwhelming. Jessica had no control over the fact that she had a learning disability. She didn't cause it. Hard work, perseverance, trained and caring teachers, and encouragement from family and friends were all a part of her journey. She strove diligently for many years and still must work harder than most to do to achieve what is considered a basic life skill. Jessica acknowledges she has limitations, but she is not defeated by them. Like Jessica, we all can do hard things with God's help.

—Beth

"One who gains strength by overcoming obstacles possesses the only strength which can overcome adversity."—Albert Schweitzer

PROMPT:

What are your limitations? What tools do you use or can you use to help you move forward?

_____

_____

_____

_____

_____

_____

_____

Who has been helpful in your journey? Make a list of ways God is helping you do hard things.

_____

_____

_____

_____

_____

_____

_____

CHAPTER 10

MENACE IN THE MILK

The Lord is a refuge for the oppressed, a stronghold in times of trouble. Those who know your name trust in you, for you, Lord, have never forsaken those who seek you. (Psalm 9:9–10)

The battle raged on, getting closer and closer to Jael's tent. As she heard the soldiers approach, she rushed to see which side was nearest. When she peeked out of the tent flap, relief flooded through her. The Israelites. Seeing leaders Deborah and Barak come into view, she stepped outside and motioned frantically for them to enter her tent.

"Barak! Deborah! He's in here. Follow me." Jael opened the flap and ducked in first. There Sisera lay, no longer the mighty warrior. A tent peg protruded from his head, blood pooling on the ground.

"What happened to him?" Barak asked.

"I killed him." Jael whispered, as if his dead body might hear her and wake up. *Maybe it was all a dream. But no, there he is.*

"Tell me how you were able to do this great deed for us." Deborah took her hand and led her outside to sit under the big cypress tree.

As soon as Sisera had come, Jael sensed she had to do something to help the Israelite army despite the panic overtaking her. She was afraid she would miss hitting the peg when she swung the hammer, and he'd end up killing her instead.

While she told Deborah her story, Jael's hands shook uncontrollably in her lap. "Sisera came to my door seeking refuge," Jael said, her hands shaking in her lap. "I said, 'Don't be afraid. I'll hide you inside my tent.' He followed me in, and I covered him with a blanket. I offered him some milk because he was thirsty and tired from running. Sisera told me to stand in the doorway and tell anyone coming by that I was alone. But instead, when he fell asleep, I grabbed a hammer and tent peg and drove the peg into his head all the way to the ground."

Deborah steadied Jael's hands with her own. "Do not be afraid. Through you, a woman like me, God provided someone to kill our worst enemy."

Do you have an "enemy" in your life? What obstacle threatens you? God is mightier than any enemy you may face today. He wants to give you the courage, strength, and knowledge needed to win any battle you find yourself in. Trust him to help you.

—Beth

"If there is no struggle, there is no progress."—Fredrick Douglass

PROMPT:

Name your enemy. Write it down. Is it anger, fear, confusion? Is it racism, prejudice, persecution? Ask God for bravery in defeating your enemy.

_____

_____

_____

_____

_____

_____

_____

Read chapters 4 and 5 of Judges for the biblical account of Jael.

CHAPTER 11

FREE INDEED: A SHOCKING DELIVERANCE

So if the Son sets you free, you will be free indeed. (John 8:36)

Shortly after we were married, Kevin and I saw a popular movie that was set in a psychiatric hospital. It included a scene where the main character received a shock treatment. Although I covered my eyes during the scene, I didn't have enough hands to cover my ears too. My heart beat wildly during the remainder of the movie. I couldn't go to sleep that night. That one horrible scene kept echoing in my brain.

My dread of mental illness—shock treatments in particular—began early.

When I was six, I overheard Mom telling a friend about sitting with my alcoholic father while he received a shock treatment. The fear that I would inherit Daddy's genes and someday need shock treatments myself was so alarming, I buried all memory of it. Seeing that movie zapped the repressed terror to life, and dread haunted me for the next two years.

Although daylight hours held little distress, nighttime was a different story. When dusk gave way to nightfall, the horrible memories would creep in. I'd close my eyes to sleep and see an orderly strapping a man to a table, followed by violent screams. Kev read the Psalms to me every night until I finally nodded off.

Even though I had been a Christian for most of my life, I saw no way to get free of the panic that imprisoned my mind.

Two years later, I watched a Christian TV interview of a lady who'd been miraculously set free from mental illness. Before that, she'd spent time in a psychiatric hospital and received dozens of shock treatments. When she started to describe how they strapped her onto the gurney to wheel her down the hall for her treatment, I panicked, bolting to the other end of the house, where Kevin sat playing the piano.

"You have to help me!" I screamed. "I can't live with this mental torment. Please do something!" Kev hugged me and prayed over me, but the ugly claws of terror still gripped my brain. I trudged back up the hallway, despairing that I'd never find relief. When I returned to the living room, I noticed a phone number for prayer scrolling across the TV screen. With my heart still hammering, I picked up the phone.

A young man listened patiently as I related my horror story. Then he said, "Ma'am, I'm going to pray with you that Jesus will heal you from this fear. But when I'm done praying, don't hang up. I have some Scriptures to share with you."

As he prayed, I felt an enormous sense of peace, like a bucket of warm honey, flow through my entire being. My heart was light and my mind calm for the first time in two years.

When the prayer ended, the young man directed me to write down a list of Scripture references, from Genesis to Revelation, about overcoming fear. "I want you to read every one of these out loud to the devil and tell him to get out and never come back," he said.

An hour or two swished by as I sat as the kitchen table and opened my Bible to the dozens of verses about not fearing. I read them aloud to the author of fear. When I finished, I closed my Bible with a slap of finality and said, "No more, Devil. You have no rights over my mind. Jesus has bought me—including my thoughts—with his blood. Leave me now, in his mighty name!"

I did not see the fear leave. I did not hear it leave. But the peace remained. Because of a kind young man's heartfelt prayer and the power in the Word of God, Jesus set me free from the suffocating waves of fear and planted my feet on the solid ground of his love.

That was nearly four decades ago. The same demon of fear has attacked me several times since then, trying to regain a foothold, to see if I meant what I said when I told the enemy to desist. When I've spoken, sung, and listened to the Word of God and refused to give in to panic, the enemy has given up every time. Thank God, the name of Jesus and the Scriptures still contain as much power and authority as they ever did to make us free indeed.

For believers, that should come as no shock.

—Jeanette

"It is not events that disturb people. It is their judgments concerning them."—Epictetus

PROMPT:

Has fear invaded your mind, choking out joy?

_____

_____

_____

_____

_____

Invite Jesus to bathe your thoughts with his deep love. Then tell Satan, "No more—get out and stay out!"

"So if the Son sets you free, you will be free indeed."

John 8:36 NIV

CHAPTER 12

SAVED FROM WITHIN THE CITY

The Lord is with me; I will not be afraid. What can mere mortals do to me? (Psalm 118:6)

Rumors flew throughout Jericho like magpies.

"Rahab, did you hear? Jewish spies are in the city. The soldiers are hunting for them everywhere."

"I heard." Rahab averted her eyes as she paid quickly for the bread in her hand. *And I know where they are.*

The two spies had knocked on her door the evening before, looking for a place to spend the night. She'd taken their money and let them in because she needed the income. *But what would happen to her if anyone found out she was harboring the enemy?*

"See you tomorrow." Rahab turned from the vendor's stall and rushed back home.

Inside, the two spies were conversing, but they turned when she dropped her food purchases onto the wooden table. One was about to greet her, but the worry lines in her forehead silenced him.

She gestured with frantic hands. "The soldiers were informed you are in the city. You need to get out tonight."

"How?" the other spy asked. "The gates will be guarded."

"I realize your God is strong. Your people win every battle you fight. But you can't stay here." Rahab walked to the window to think.

When she turned back toward the men, she said, "I have a plan that might work. Since my house is built in the city wall, I could lower you down with a rope. Then you run to the hills and hide until its safe." Her eyes sparkled with cautious excitement.

"Are you sure you want to put yourself in danger?" The man looked deep into her eyes until Rahab nodded. "Do this for us," he continued, "and we will protect you. When we invade, tie this scarlet cord in your window where we can see it. We will keep you and whoever is in this home safe."

"You'll need to hide on the roof until dark," she said. "I will cover you with the stalks of flax drying up there."

As the sun set, she heard pounding on her door as harsh voices demanded, "Where are the spies? We were told they're here."

Rahab bit her lip and whispered, "Lord of the Israelites, protect us." Terror squeezed her chest as she opened the door. Two soldiers barged in.

"They were here, but left," she said. "I thought they were simply travelers. I don't know where they went."

"We don't believe you." The soldiers began searching through her small rooms that contained her meager possessions. They climbed the steps to the roof. Rahab held her breath. *Had she hidden the spies well enough? Would a protruding foot or errant bit of cloth reveal their presence? Would the soldier move the flax?* A moment later soldiers thundered back down the stairs out of her house.

She leaned against the inside of the door, and then slid down as her legs gave way. Only then did the tears of relief fall. She gulped air, trying to calm her emotions.

The spies silently moved down the stairs and helped Rahab up. Then, as they all waited for the sun to set, they gathered around the table and ate bread and cheese.

During the darkest hours of the night when Jericho's residents were asleep and even the soldiers standing guard were fighting drowsiness, Rahab leaned out her window and silently let down a length of rope. The Jewish spies climbed down quickly and quietly. Rahab held her breath as she watched them descend. Then she pulled the rope back up, whispering a prayer to the God of the Israelites, whoever he was. Her heart didn't return to a more regular rhythm until she saw the men finally make it to the woods and disappear without being pursued.

Months later, the Israelite army advanced on the city. Rahab gathered her family into her home and hung the prearranged red cord out the window. The army marched for six days while people inside the city cowered in fear. Finally, on the seventh day, the massive city wall collapsed without the Israelite army using any force. All the Israelites had to do was walk in and invade. As the battle raged and her people fell, Rahab waited.

Soon a knock came at her door. The spies had returned, as they'd promised, to take her and her loved ones to safety.

At times, our impossible situations may require us to trust God for a miracle. At other times, we may need to take a stand against evil ourselves. Sometimes, we need to do both. When Rahab trusted in a God she had no knowledge of, that God used her and rewarded her. The first chapter of Matthew reveals that she went on to become the great-great-grandmother of King David. God will answer our prayers and protect us when we defend his people and his name, just like he did for Rahab.

—Beth

"What worries you, masters you."—John Locke

PROMPT:

Are you frightened to do the right thing? To defend God's name? To defend his people? To protect someone from harm? Write a prayer to God, asking him for strength and courage.

Read Joshua 2 and 6 for the biblical account of Rahab. Matthew 1:5 shows her lineage.

CHAPTER 13

FRIENDS: MANNA FROM HEAVEN

When I am afraid, I put my trust in you. (Psalm 56:3)

Susan stared into space, her knuckles white, her jaw clenched. The news was devastating. "It's malignant. Breast cancer."

The aroma of chili cooking on the stove mocked her lost appetite on that cold Monday night in October. At forty years old, Susan worried about her two young daughters, just six and three. *God, let me see my girls grow up,* she silently pleaded. *Also, I'll need encouragement every day if I'm to make it through this. A phone call, a card, anything.*

Susan asked God for his presence so she would sense he was with her, and without fail, every single day, God gave her the help she'd asked for.

Outside the door at the first doctor's appointment, her friend DeeDee hugged her. "Suz, I'll be there with you through it all, at every doctor's appointment, whenever you need me." And she kept that promise. She sat beside Susan in every waiting room, and the rest of the time consistently checked in by phone.

Some days, friends picked up the kids to give Susan a break. Other friends called to pray with her.

Peggy cleaned her house. When Susan's daughters brought lice home from school—three times—Joy picked the insects out of Susan's hair.

Even the lice infestation turned out to be a gift from God. As Susan stuffed a seemingly unending parade of bed sheets into the washer, she cried out to God, "Why? Why lice, Lord? I'm so tired." She heard God whisper, "The lice prevent you from worrying about the cancer." God kept her so busy living, she was unable to stop and let the worry take over.

Cynthia gave Susan a card filled with Scriptures, which Susan kept in her Bible years after the cancer was gone, a reminder of God's faithfulness and the blessing of godly friendships.

Susan and her friend Melody met halfway between each other's homes for lunch. As they hugged and cried together, Melody told her, "I have something for you." She pulled out a painting she had created for Susan depicting a chair in the middle of a flower garden. Susan hung that picture in a prominent place in her home where it could remind her of the love and prayers of her special friend.

Other friends would call to pray or give her a Scripture to read. She sensed God's nearness through friends and family. Through the dark moments, Susan clung to Psalm 56:3: "For when I am afraid, I will trust in you."

It was a wonderful day when she received good news from the doctor, "We got it all. No chemo, no radiation, no pills needed."

Today, Susan has been cancer-free for nineteen years. What she gained from the ordeal is the memory of God's presence through all the tears, the fatigue, and the laughter and joy when she learned the surgeon had gotten it all. God was with her every moment, every single day. And her friends served as a lens to see him with when she was too discouraged to perceive him herself.

—Beth

"There is nothing on this earth more to be prized than true friendship."—Thomas Aquinas

PROMPT:

How have you seen God's presence in your difficult moments? Has he worked through friends? Write down some ways you have seen God at work in your life.

_____

_____

_____

_____

_____

_____

_____

CHAPTER 14

SPICE GIRLS

For no one is cast off by the Lord forever. Though he brings grief, he will show compassion, so great is his unfailing love. For he does not willingly bring affliction or grief to anyone. (Lamentations 3: 31–33)

"Here, Johanna. You carry this jar. I'll take the larger one." Mary held out a small container of spices meant for preparing a body for burial.

Quietly they left the house and headed down the dirt path toward the graves, with only the first light of daybreak as illumination. Other women, true believers of Jesus, joined along the way. Lines of sadness and worry etched their faces. Jesus had died, and they were uncertain about what would happen to their group of followers. But they recognized their next step. Applying spices to Jesus's body would be their last act of love and devotion to the man they had believed was the Messiah. But now he was dead—a lifeless body in a tomb.

They walked closely together in the cold, helping each other along the path. Most wept quietly. One stared sightlessly straight ahead. Another watched cautiously for those who were arresting followers. The last few days had been a terrible ordeal. It was unbearable to watch Jesus be arrested, tried in court, and then executed on the cross. The women sought solace from each other.

As they turned the corner to face the tomb, they expected a sealed tomb—instead the stone at the entrance had been rolled away.

In confusion, the women exclaimed, "Look!" "Oh no!" "What happened?" "What should we do?" "Should we tell someone?"

Out of the darkness two men—angels—approached.

"Where did you come from?" Johanna asked, shielding her eyes from the brilliance of their robes.

"Why are you looking for the living here among the dead?" one replied. "Look inside the tomb. Jesus isn't there."

"All I see are his clothes" Mary said, weeping. "Where did they take him?"

"Jesus is risen. Go tell the others."

With minds still full of questions, the women ran off to tell the disciples what they had seen.

Soon the risen Lord Jesus began appearing to other believers. But this little band of women, true believers weighed down by grief, was the first to learn of the resurrected Jesus.

God deeply loves us all. He cares for the brokenhearted. Are you in the middle of a grieving period? Have you lost someone you love? Or has a dream died? Do you have a group of friends to lean on in your grief?

—Beth

One who knows how to show and to accept kindness will be a friend better than any possession. —Sophocles

PROMPT:

What you are grieving? Make a list of those you can lean on. What can you do to reach out for support?

_____

_____

_____

_____

_____

_____

_____

Is there someone who needs to lean on you? Name one thing you can do to support that friend.

_____

_____

_____

_____

_____

_____

Read Luke 24:1–12 for the biblical account of the spice girls.

CHAPTER 15

A FRIENDLY SURPRISE

Let us then approach God's throne of grace with confidence, so that we may receive mercy and find grace to help us in our time of need. (Hebrews 4:16)

"Lord, I need someone to talk to—someone who's been through a similar challenge and who's objective. Please bring such a person to mind."

Four years earlier, my ninety-year-old mom had moved from across the county to live in our town. During Kevin's and my forty years of marriage up to this time, we had led a fairly quiet life. That ended the day Mom moved near us.

It wasn't only the questions about our private lives she'd asked over the past forty-eight months. Or continual requests that we stop by her place to help her find missing items. Those simply annoyed us and took time. But lately, I'd grown concerned over more serious issues.

Mom never wanted to use her cane or walker—in spite of several recent falls. Once she even broke some ribs. She often forgot what had happened that morning or what day of the week it was. My mother was failing. And I didn't know what to do.

"Call Katie," a gentle voice in my heart whispered. Katie was a friend from church whose mother had Alzheimer's. Katie had cared for her mom until it was no longer safe to leave her alone in her home. Katie was forced to put her mother into a memory care facility.

Aha, Katie is the perfect person to help. She'll be able to offer me the comfort and advice I need. I eagerly dialed her work number, hoping we could get together that day for lunch. When I explained my plight, Katie was sympathetic, but pressed for time.

"I'm so swamped, I can't get away till next month," she said. "Can you wait that long?"

I told her sure, not a problem. Inwardly, I was disappointed. Who was going to help me in the meantime? I prepared to say goodbye, but then Katie began to tell me her own story.

"Mom has a huge bruise on her arm," she said. "The nurses think it might be a blood clot, but they have no idea how she got it." Her voice was heavy with fatigue and worry. "One of the other residents told me Mom tries to escape every day. I know she hates living there, but I had no choice." Katie explained how she had to take off work to drive her mom to the emergency room, and then make up her missed work hours later in the week.

"Don't your two brothers who live here help you?" I asked.
"Not that much."

Even though I was the only child left since my brother had died, at least my husband and two kids pitched in to help with Mom. It seemed Katie's situation was far worse than mine.

I promised to pray for Katie and her mom. She thanked me with a smile in her voice.

The next Sunday at church, Katie told me her mom's arm was beginning to heal.

"My mom's ribs are starting to give her less pain, too," I replied. We stood and chatted longer than usual. I realized

Katie needed a friend with whom she could share her concerns, just as much as I did. I'd thought the Lord was leading me to her because she could solve some of my problems. Instead, he surprised me with the gift of a new friendship.

—Jeanette

"You may forget with whom you laughed, but you will never forget with whom you wept." —Kahlil Gibran

Prompt:

Do you have a loved one who's failing physically or mentally? Tell God about it.

_____

_____

_____

_____

_____

_____

_____

Ask the Lord of all mercy to help you find someone to share your burdens with.

_____

_____

_____

_____

_____

_____

_____

CHAPTER 16

SOMEONE TO STAND BY ME

A friend loves at all times, and a brother is born for a time of adversity. (Proverbs 17:17)

God, why have you forsaken me? At least it certainly feels like you have. What am I to do now? I'm all alone.

Naomi wrestled with grief and depression. First, she'd lost her husband, and then her two sons had died. And now, an immigrant, she was left in a foreign town, far from family, without any way to get by. Solutions seemed to be beyond reach. Naomi let the sadness overtake her.

Have you ever felt like Naomi? Overwhelmed? Without hope? With no answers in sight? In Naomi's grief, she asked to be called Mara, which means bitter. She had decided she was abandoned by God. In her eyes, her life was over. When she had left for Moab with a husband and children, her life had been full of hope and dreams for a future. Now, as she prepared to return to her homeland, she was empty-handed and alone.

But God wasn't finished with Naomi or her story. He intertwined her life narrative with that of her daughter-in-law, Ruth, a native of the foreign land Naomi had lived in for so long.

The story unfolded when, in the middle of her bitterness, Naomi told Ruth to stay in Moab with her own people.

To that, Ruth replied, "Where you go I will go, and where you stay I will stay. Your people will be my people and your God my God. Where you die I will die, and there I will be buried. May the Lord deal with me, be it ever so severely, if even death separates you and me" (Ruth 1:16–17). In other words, when Naomi tried to push Ruth away, Ruth remained faithfully by her side anyway.

And so they began their lifelong journey together. At the start, it looked like their lives would be bleak and difficult. But God had different plans. He gave Ruth to Naomi to be a confidante to lean on and someone who would give her strength and encouragement. The Lord provided safety on their trip to Israel, food for the winter, and eventually a husband for Ruth, who would care for Naomi also.

God even remembered Naomi's loss, and through Ruth, gave her a grandson to love and care for. "The women said to Naomi: 'Praise be to the Lord, who this day has not left you without a guardian-redeemer. May he become famous throughout Israel! He will renew your life and sustain you in your old age. For your daughter-in-law, who loves you and who is better to you than seven sons, has given him birth'" (Ruth 4:14–15).

Do you feel alone? Are you at a crossroads? Have life's circumstances left you empty? Are you struggling with depression or bitterness? Look around you and see who is by your side. Who is that unexpected person standing with you when everyone else has fled? Who continues to walk with you? And remember. Even if no human companion remains by your side, rest assured that God is still with you.

—Beth

"One does nothing who tries to console a despondent person with words. A friend is one who aids with deeds at a critical time when deeds are called for."—Euripides

PROMPT:

Journal about a friend who has helped you when you are discouraged. Then write that friend a note of gratitude.

_____

_____

_____

_____

_____

_____

_____

Read the book of Ruth for the biblical account of Naomi.

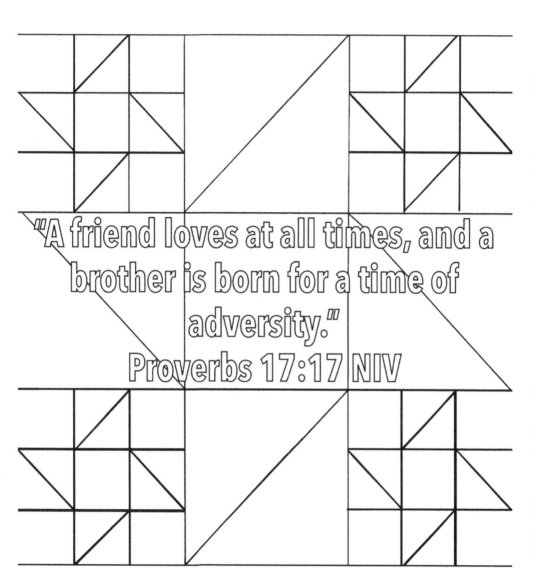

"A friend loves at all times, and a brother is born for a time of adversity."
Proverbs 17:17 NIV

CHAPTER 17

FINDING PURPOSE THROUGH PAIN

Have I not commanded you? Be strong and courageous.
Do not be afraid; do not be discouraged, for the Lord
your God will be with you wherever you go. (Joshua 1:9)

Teresa sat holding the hand of her mother, Joy, who had
been diagnosed with brain cancer in January. Now a mere
four months later, the once-beautiful woman was in her final
days, her lovely face now horribly swollen as a side effect
of medication. At one time she'd been a helper, entertainer,
and servant-minded woman, but now she was the one being
taken care of. Yet as cancer ravished her brain, she maintained
her gentle spirit and a strong faith in God.

Teresa took family medical leave from her job to assist
her dad who was her mother's primary caregiver. The job was
exhausting, both physically and emotionally, as she tried to
be present for her sick mother. But the hospice social worker
helped Teresa navigate the difficult unknowns.

As snow fell one late winter day, Joy said to Teresa, "One
day you will tell people about this." Her words foreshadowed
how God would use Teresa's experience with death and grief,
because Joy's death wasn't the only difficult situation she
would find herself in.

Soon after Joy's death, the health of Teresa's Grandfather
McCallum declined rapidly due to congestive heart failure

and COPD. As Teresa sat beside his bed, he told her, "God has a plan for you." Her grieving heart ached even more. She was losing one of her biggest cheerleaders.

Once more hospice came to help the grieving family. Just a few weeks after his rapid decline, her grandfather died the way he lived, trusting God, calmly and patiently.

Only seven weeks later, her other grandfather passed away.

Hospice was again a comforting presence throughout the last year of Teresa's mother-in-law's battle with Alzheimer's. Unforeseen needs were met, such as when the hospice chaplain spent hours singing with the ill woman, and a volunteer washed and styled her hair to give Teresa's father-in-law time to run errands. During the final months, a social worker helped the family transition her mother-in-law into an Alzheimer's facility.

As difficult as these experiences were for Teresa, God gave her a special gift, a sense of leading. "Each of these experiences confirmed my interest in hospice care," she says. "I was able to learn and understand more about the dying process, as well as how grief (and anticipatory grief) can affect families. I was reaffirmed in my spirit that I enjoy hospice care and caring for others who are nearing the end of life."

When her youngest child went off to college, Teresa registered for classes to get a master's degree in social work. Soon Teresa will be blessing others the way she was blessed during her darkest days of grief.

God's presence and the help of the trained hospice staff during the deaths of her mother, grandfathers, and mother-in-law, revealed God's purpose for Teresa's future. God gave her hope for the future and a calling to help others on their journey through sickness and sorrow.

Will you turn your difficult journey over to God and let him use it to define your future? He can use your heartache for good if you will let him.

—Beth

"I am not afraid of storms, for I am learning how to sail my ship."—Louisa May Alcott

PROMPT:

How can God use your pain to help others? List some things you can do to help others going through situations you have already experienced.

_____

_____

_____

_____

_____

_____

_____

_____

_____

_____

_____

_____

_____

CHAPTER 18

MAKING THE HARD DECISIONS

As for God, his way is perfect: The Lord's word is flawless; he shields all who take refuge in him. (Psalm 18:30)

"I'm going with you to Bethlehem."

When her mother-in-law, Naomi, told her to turn around and go back to her parents, Ruth stood her ground. Although it was dangerous for two widowed women to travel alone, she discerned the decision was right. When she had married into Naomi's family, Ruth discovered that the Israelites lived differently than her Moabite family. Her husband's family was honest, kind, and hardworking. They introduced her to the one true God. She realized she could never go back to living a Moabite lifestyle.

After days of hard travel, the two arrived in Bethlehem, Naomi's hometown. Women ran to greet Naomi—family and friends she hadn't seen in years. All the hugs proved to Ruth that she had made the right choice to come along. Now she just needed to think of a way to help the two of them survive.

"Naomi, would it be safe for me to pick up leftover grain at the edges of the fields?" Ruth asked as they prepared for bed that night.

"Yes, my daughter," said Naomi, sounding surprised at Ruth's resourcefulness.

Early the next morning, Ruth was picking up grain in a field that belonged to a man named Boaz. After discovering that Ruth was Naomi's daughter-in-law, and therefore a relative, Boaz told her to stay in his field and pick grain alongside his workers. He protected her from unsavory men and instructed his harvesters to make sure extra grain was left in the area where she was working. Ruth gathered steadily, and soon it was lunchtime. Ruth sat a few feet away from Boaz's workers. As she listened to the group's friendly banter, she felt the pangs of loneliness and homesickness.

"Come eat with us." Boaz handed Ruth some roasted grain. "I've noticed how kind you have been to Naomi. May our God keep you safe and bless you for your willingness to leave family and homeland to care for Naomi."

A woman patted the ground beside her, and Ruth moved closer. A little bit of the homesickness lessened.

At the end of the day, Ruth rushed home to share her good news with Naomi. "I worked in Boaz's field. He was kind and generous to me."

"The Lord be blessed," Naomi responded, explaining that Boaz was a good man and would do all he could to make the women's future secure.

In fact, Boaz and Ruth soon married, giving the two women a family again. Soon Ruth gave birth to a son, whom they named Obed. He had a son named Jesse, who had a son named David, the king of Israel. God blessed Ruth for her decision to choose faith in him and loyalty to her mother-in-law instead of remaining where everything was familiar.

At times, our life journey forces us to make hard decisions. Ruth made a difficult one when she left her family of origin to travel with her mother-in-law and live in a city where Ruth knew no one.

Have you ever had to leave those familiar and loved? Have you left a life that was comfortable and safe? Maybe because of a marriage, a divorce, a death, a job, or schooling? Like Ruth, perhaps you fear the future. Can you trust in God for your future?

—Beth

"Decision is a risk rooted in the courage of being free."—Paul Tillich

PROMPT:

Are you facing a hard decision—or have you had to make one? List some ways God is helping you walk into the future.

_____

_____

_____

_____

_____

_____

_____

Read the book of Ruth for the biblical account of this godly woman.

CHAPTER 19

A Moving Miracle

Yet the LORD longs to be gracious to you; therefore he will rise up to show you compassion. (Isaiah 30:18)

Since Dirk never allowed Mariah to work, she'd been a stay-at-home-mom for twelve years, homeschooling their three kids. So when Dirk filed for divorce, she was devastated. He'd proved to be unreliable about paying bills. Would he give her child support? If not, what would she do? Could she find a job that paid her enough to support four people?

Eventually Mariah landed a job in a grocery store and found a two-bedroom apartment in a tolerable neighborhood. After a few months, the child support checks stopped. Mariah had to apply for food assistance, sign up the kids for free school lunches, and even accept Christmas gifts from Angel Tree. She'd grown up in a Christian home and witnessed many instances of God providing for their needs when funds were low. But she never imagined she'd need to rely on the government for her children's food. Where was God when she needed him most?

Dirk had visitation rights two nights a week and two weekends a month. He took the kids out to dinner and bought them expensive gifts, but thwarted Mariah's attempts to raise them as God-fearing people. And he continued to withhold child support.

After a year of living paycheck to paycheck, with never enough time for her family, Mariah decided to petition the court to move near her parents three states away. She longed to have extra hands to help with the kids, along with the benefit of her mom and dad's loving influence. The judge refused. She was distraught but not completely surprised. Only nine times in the 250-year history of the state she lived in had a judge allowed a mother to move her children out of state while the father remained behind.

Meanwhile, the Lord took excellent care of Mariah and her children. On Mother's Day, a stranger in a gift shop gave her a one-hundred-dollar bill. Her church family took up offerings for her and gave her clothes and shoes. Her parents sent money each month to pay for a counselor and internet service.

But Mariah was weary of raising her kids alone. Not only did she bear the financial burden of a family of four, she was also grappling with all the emotional and physical issues her children had developed. In addition, she suffered from PTSD and polymyalgia rheumatica, a painful muscle disease that made it difficult to walk and move. She needed a miracle.

At the end of year two, Dirk was $40,000 in arrears on child support. Mariah decided to go back to court and ask the judge to reconsider. Scores of people all over the nation were praying that God would move the judge's heart to say yes.

Mariah's parents drove eight hours to be with her on the day of the court hearing. At the end of several grueling hours of deliberation and arguments on the part of both attorneys, the judge awarded Mariah the right to move out of state with her children.

God showed her compassion, and against all odds, gave her the desire of her heart.

—Jeanette

"We all have the power to make wishes come true, as long as we keep believing."—Louisa May Alcott

Do you need a miracle for your family that odds say will never happen? Write your request in the lines below.

_____

_____

_____

_____

_____

_____

_____

Find some Scriptures that show how God loves to do the impossible. Write them below. Over the next few weeks, memorize them and visualize them happening in your situation.

_____

_____

_____

_____

_____

_____

_____

_____

_____

_____

_____

_____

CHAPTER 20

LAUGHING AT THE TRUTH

Wait for the Lord; be strong and take heart and wait for the Lord. (Psalm 27:14)

What would you do with an unfulfilled promise? Have you had to wait for an answer that never seemed to come?

When Abraham was ninety-nine, the Lord told him he would be the father of a great nation. His wife, Sarah, was just five years younger. She had not been able to get pregnant. Not once had she held a child of her own in her arms.

"Isn't it too late for me? How can a woman my age have a baby? This is ridiculous, Abraham," Sarah muttered when Abraham told her of God's promise. The pain of childlessness had seared a hard shell around her heart. In her old age, she'd accepted the reality of never bearing a child. Now Abraham wanted to rip open old wounds. She wasn't going to let that happen.

Later, in a vision, the Lord told Abraham again, "Look up at the sky and count the stars—if indeed you can count them … So shall your offspring be" (Genesis 15:5). Sarah heard Abraham's voice and his absurd words. She knew better than to believe the futile promise.

Finally, the Lord appeared to Abraham a third time. On this occasion, Sarah stood behind the flap of her tent and heard the crazy conversation taking place outside. She laughed and thought, Is he really saying I will have the joy of giving birth? I'm too old. It's impossible.

But the Lord heard her laughter and perceived her thoughts. He asked Abraham, "Is anything too hard for the Lord?" (Genesis 18:14).

Sure enough, just as the Lord had promised, the impossible happened. Sarah gave birth to a son in her old age. Abraham and Sarah became the parents of Isaac, through whom the nation of Israel was established.

God can turn our broken, discarded, unbelievable dreams into possibilities. Rest assured that if he made a promise, he will fulfill it. We may have to wait—sometimes for a long time. And waiting can be hard. Believing what seems like an impossibility feels ridiculous. But God wants us to trust him.

Do you have an unfulfilled promise? Or an unanswered prayer? Remember, God is the God of impossible situations.

—Beth

Good character is not formed in a week or a month. It is created little by little, day by day. Protracted and patient effort is needed to develop character. —Heraclitus

PROMPT:

What promise are you waiting on? What answer to prayer do you long for? As you color this verse, try memorizing it for comfort while you wait.

_____

_____

_____

_____

_____

_____

Read chapters 12, 15, 18, and 21 of Genesis for the biblical account of Sarah.

Wait on the Lord; be strong and take heart and and wait on the Lord. -Psalms 27:14

CHAPTER 21

HOLD THE PRECIOUS LIGHTLY

But those who hope in the Lord will renew their strength. They will soar on wings like eagles; they will run and not grow weary, they will walk and not be faint. (Isaiah 40:31)

Michael was just eighteen months old when he got what the doctor said was a virus that would pass in a day or two. But the next day, Michael was even more listless. Barb, his terrified mom, called her neighbor and friend, Mary Felice. "Will you watch Carissa and SaraBeth while I take Michael back to the doctor?" Barb twisted the phone cord in her shaky hands.

After leaving her two older children with Mary Felice, Barb sped to the doctor's office. With a determined stride, she marched up to the receptionist's window. "This baby is very sick," she said. "It's more than a virus."

"The doctor has appointments all day. He can't see you," the receptionist replied, barely looking her way.

Barb's motherly intuition took over. She declared, "I'm afraid Michael is dying. I'm staying right here until the doctor will see him again." With Michael in her arms, she sat on the only available seat, which was a padded bench under the coat rack, directly across from the receptionist's window.

Thirty minutes later, the nurse came out and took Barb and Michael to an examination room.

As soon as the doctor saw Michael, he said, "Get this baby to the ER immediately. He may have spinal meningitis, a life-threatening disease. I will call the hospital and give the staff instructions on what to do. You need to be informed that a spinal tap is the only way to determine a diagnosis. However, a spinal tap is very painful and can result in permanent damage."

At the hospital, Michael was taken to a room where the spinal tap was performed. Barb squirmed when she heard Michael's cries, and fears flooded her mind as she thought back to their recent visit to the zoo. *Could Michael have been exposed there?* But really, she had no way of discovering where her sick son had been exposed to the disease.

For several days Barb, her husband, Dennis, and Barb's mother sat at the hospital with Michael. Meanwhile, Barb's neighbor, Mary Felice, along with Barb's mother-in-law, Roberta, and sister, Beth, took turns watching seven-year-old Carissa and four-year-old SaraBeth. At first Michael was in a bland, tan-colored hospital room but was soon moved to intensive care with a windowed wall so the staff could monitor him. Barb sat in a wooden rocking chair beside the glass box containing her precious quarantined son. IV tubes ran from his motionless body. His legs were tied to a board to prevent him from jerking the port out of his ankle.

As Barb sat with Michael, she realized that death, hearing loss, and even permanent brain damage were possible realities. But she remembered back to his birth. Michael had been a preemie with his umbilical cord wrapped around his throat. If he had not been born until he was full term, he might have been dead or brain damaged. As Barb sat watching Michael again in peril, she told God that Michael was his, not theirs, and that his life was still in God's hands.

She sang to Michael the song, "They That Wait," encouraging herself and those around her with this promise from Isaiah 40:31 (KJV):

> They that wait upon the LORD shall renew their strength;
> they shall mount up with wings as eagles; they shall run,
> and not be weary; they shall walk, and not faint.

The last line of the song she sang was a request for the Lord to teach her to wait.

God had given Barb a sweet peace at the moment of Michael's birth, and he did so again during the time Michael spent in intensive care with spinal meningitis. A few days later, Michael improved enough to be moved to the pediatric area. Tears of thankfulness ran down Barb's face as she realized her son was going to make it. Later that week, she carried her recovered son out of the dark, dreary hospital and into summer sunlight.

"If God wants me to have what is precious in my life, it will come to me and it will remain until God releases it from me," she said, a discerning smile gracing her face. Michael is now an adult, and Barb reminds him often that God has his hand on him.

—Beth

"God sweetens outward pain with inward peace."—Thomas Watson

PROMPT:

Have you experienced inner peace during times of outer pain? Write about how that peace helped you deal with your pain.

_____

_____

_____

_____

_____

_____

_____

CHAPTER 22

A BABY AMONG CROCODILES

May the Lord answer you when you are in distress; may the name of the God of Jacob protect you. (Psalm 20:1)

What would you do if your child was threatened or your family was in danger? How far would you go to protect them?

Jochebed faced those questions. Her Hebrew family was enslaved by the Egyptians. The Egyptian king was afraid that if the Israelite population got too large, they would revolt, so he issued a new decree stating that all Hebrew baby boys were to be killed.

Jochebed was worried because she had just delivered a son. The only way she could think of to keep her baby alive was to put him in a watertight basket in the Nile River and hope he would float away to safety.

So, she did that and placed Moses's older sister in tall reeds near the basket. "Stay here and watch," Jochebed told her daughter. "Tell me what happens." Wiping away tears, she turned her back on her precious baby and walked away. As a slave, she had work requirements. The overseer would notice if she didn't show up for work.

Sometime after she left, Pharaoh's daughter came to bathe. When she saw the basket bobbing in the gentle waves, she told one of her attendants to retrieve it.

The baby began to cry.

"Shh. Poor baby, you must be a Hebrew child," the princess said as she lifted Moses from his watery bed and held him close. "I will name him Moses because I plucked him out of the water."

His sister rushed out of her hiding place to stop the princess as she made her way to the opposite shore. "My mother can nurse him for you."

Because of the girl's quick thinking, Jochebed not only received news that her son was saved, but she was also able to love, care for him, and teach him about his people and his God until he was weaned.

Her little son, marked for death, was raised in a palace. God would use him to deliver the Israelite people out of slavery in Egypt and lead them to the promised land of Israel.

How horrible for Jochebed to watch her child's life in danger. Have you ever experienced that moment when the phone rang, and your heart skipped a beat?

Does your child have a serious illness? Have you dropped your kids off at college or helped them move into their first apartment? Motherhood is not for the faint of heart. It often comes with of sadness, worry, or regret, along with out-of-control situations and times when your heart is about to break in two. In those moments, take a step toward the heavenly Father. Let him hold you and your child.
—**Beth**

"[God] will never cease to help us until we cease to need."—Charles Spurgeon

Name a situation in your life that appears out of your control. Ask God to give you the ability to lean into him and let go of your tight grip. Write the situation or name on a piece of paper and hold it in your hands. Lift your hands and give God permission to take care of what you've been clutching so tightly. Now leave your hands open and turn them palms down as you give to God what falls from your hands.

_____
_____
_____
_____
_____
_____
_____

Read chapters 1 and 2 of Exodus for the biblical account of Jochebed.

CHAPTER 23

FROM BLING TO BLESSED

Jesus looked at them and said, "With man this is impossible, but with God all things are possible." (Matthew 19:26)

I stared at the gaping hole in my engagement ring where my diamond should have been, then at the broken prong that had allowed the loss. That emptiness reflected the way my heart felt.

The love that my husband, Kevin, and I pledged to each other twenty-five years earlier had lost its shine, leaving disappointment and neglect in its place. Fun dates, long phone conversations, and shared dreams had taken a backseat to our careers. And now that our kids had moved out, it seemed Kevin and I had little in common.

"Lord," I prayed, "please bring back the sparkle we once shared. I know it's not your will for us to live like strangers in the same house. Knit our hearts together, like the apostle Paul prayed in Colossians 2:2 (KJV)."

When we'd chosen the ring a week after our engagement, we'd picked a setting of one simple diamond nestled in the center of a white-gold rose on a band of antique-gold leaves. Now the diamond was lost down a shower drain or lying in a sewer somewhere. When I realized I wasn't grieving over it like I should have, I sighed.

At least now I can finally have the ring I've always wanted with lots of color and bling. After I made an appointment to see a jeweler, I planned my pitch to Kevin, praying that he'd agree to my idea of a flashy design.

But he was crushed. "That's the ring we picked out together, Jeanette. It reminds me of the excitement we shared when we were first married. I hate the thought of replacing it with a different ring—one that has no history."

Although his response gave me a glimmer of hope for our future, I was still determined to have my way. *I'll just wait till we visit the jewelry store, then I'll ooh and ahh over whatever ring has the most bling. Surely, Kevin won't refuse my request in front of a stranger.*

When the jeweler asked to see my empty setting, I said, "I'd like to look at other styles. We've been married so long—I'm ready for something new."

He smiled and nodded. "Go right ahead. But in case you change your mind, I'll take this one in the back and see if I have a diamond that fits."

Kevin stayed quiet, his eyes avoiding mine.

Just as I'd planned, I raved over emeralds and sapphires in the most elaborate settings available. Soon the jeweler returned. "I'm sure this stone will fit your setting," he said as he placed a black velvet pillow in front of us. On it sat the most stunning diamond I'd ever seen, its shape and size nearly identical to my missing stone, its facets shimmering with a thousand colors.

As I gazed down at this lovely prism, a flash of truth stirred my heart. *I don't need a fancy new ring. I have a solid, faithful setting that needs only a finer stone to give it new life. This assures me that Jesus will show us how to add the bling we need to make our marriage sparkle again too.* God had answered my prayer in a way that surprised me—by changing my heart. I realized that what I wanted was what I'd had all along.

"We'll take it," I said to the jeweler as I slipped my hand in Kevin's. When I caught the glimmer of renewed love in his eyes, my hope for our future shone brighter than ever.

—**Jeanette**

"Some of us think holding on makes us strong but sometimes it is letting go."—Hermann Hesse

Brainstorm a few ways God could bring new life to a relationship that's grown stale.

_____

_____

_____

_____

_____

_____

_____

Now, give God permission to fix it however he likes.

Thank you for choosing me.

CHAPTER 24

What Now?

*You who are simple, gain prudence; you who are foolish,
set your hearts on it. (Proverbs 8:5)*

Abigail watched as dark clouds marched across the sky
in her direction. Where she stood was still a beautiful day,
but she could see the storm coming. And it looked like more
than a simple thunderstorm.

At that moment, the head shepherd rushed toward her.
Oh no, she thought. *What has my husband done now?*

"Abigail, we need your help. David sent messengers to
greet our master, but Nabal insulted them and turned them
away. Now we fear disaster. David's warriors will cut us all
down unless you can stop them." He was out of breath from
exertion and fear. His eyes darted back and forth as if he were
on the alert for men with spears to pop up over the next hill.

Acting quickly, Abigail wrapped up all the bread, fruit,
and beverages planned for the workers' supper and loaded
the supplies on donkeys. Then she and her workers headed
out to meet the attackers.

Now to accomplish this without Nabal's knowledge. Beads
of perspiration formed at the thought of what her husband
would do if he learned of her plan.

The men with the donkeys led the way. She tried calming
her swirling thoughts by watching the donkeys' tails flip back

and forth. But soon she looked up the mountain trail and saw the realization of her worst fear. David and his army of soldiers approached.

Oh, God, didn't this man just say he had been repaid evil for all the good he had done protecting our sheep? Didn't he tell my men he would kill us all? Panic squeezed her chest.

Abigail jumped off her donkey, bowed before David, and fell at his feet. "Please, don't pay any attention to anything Nabal says," she begged. "He is a foolish man, just like his name says. I recognize you; the future king of Israel. God has given you success everywhere. Spare us so your conscience will remain clean." She turned and gestured toward the donkeys behind her. "I bring gifts for your men."

David received the items she'd brought as a peace offering. "You may return home," he said. "You are safe from me and my men." Then he led his warriors away.

Abigail sat on the hard ground, breathed deeply, and looked up at the sky. Rain clouds still headed their way, but disaster had been averted.

Back home, Abigail discovered Nabal in the middle of hosting a banquet. Wine flowed freely, and laughter filled the room. Now was not the time to tell Nabal about the narrowly averted consequences of his foolish actions. So she quietly slipped out of the party and went back to her room for the evening.

When Nabal sobered up the next day, Abigail told him the whole story. The shock of what he had nearly done was too much for his alcohol-abused body. He had a stroke and lingered, paralyzed, for ten days until he died.

What a difficult situation for Abigail! No doubt this was not the first foolish thing Nabal had done, but it was probably the worst. The Bible doesn't tell us all the other ways Abigail had to smooth over problems he'd caused. Although her life had been one of wealth, it was also one of constant turmoil with a foolish drunk for a husband.

Like Abigail, sometimes we find ourselves in situations we didn't cause and involved with people who fill our lives with drama and require us to be problem-solvers. Abigail probably thought, "No, not again!"

Have you ever whispered those words under your breath? In every difficult relationship we face, God can teach us, guide us, and provide us with the wisdom we need. Trust him today with your hard relationships.

—Beth

"As I grow older, I pay less attention to what men say. I just watch what they do."—Andrew Carnegie

PROMPT:

Do you have a "Nabal" in your life? If so, how is God refining you as you learn to relate to this difficult person?

_____

_____

_____

_____

_____

_____

Read chapter 25 of 1 Samuel for the biblical account of Abigail.

CHAPTER 25

HUGS FROM DAD AND FATHER

The angel of the Lord encamps around those who fear him, and he delivers them. (Psalm 34:7)

Jen stood to leave, but her dad pointed to her, then to her mom, and back to himself. Throat cancer had robbed him of his voice, but his eyes told her exactly what he wanted, for the three of them to stay together a little longer, so she spent a sleepless night in the recliner next to him.

Her jeans-and-cowboy-boots father had been the epitome of a man's man. He'd spent his free time gardening, fishing, and hunting with his Bluetick Coonhounds. Now, instead of the smell of the oilfield on his skin, the sad odor of disinfectant filled the air.

In her mind, she could almost taste the delicious potato soup he used to make for the family. She remembered him waking her to watch the movie *Yankee Doodle Dandy*. He had become her dad when she was just a toddler, filling her childhood with security and her teenage years with fights. Too soon he would be gone, and she would be fatherless again. Never a huggy, I-love-you kind of family, they were all changed by his cancer diagnosis. During his final days, the family drew together and found strength in each other's arms.

Then one year later, almost to the day of Jen's dad's death, her mother called with news. "Jen, hon, lung cancer has metastasized to my right leg." As a nurse, Jen's mom understood the diagnosis. She was dying.

As Jen drove each day to the rehab facility, she thought back over the past four years and how she and her mother had become friends on an adult level. She smiled, remembering when they'd giggled like schoolgirls the first time her mom had been able to drive her car after her leg had healed from surgery. Jen loved how her soft-spoken mom could really express her opinion when asked. *How does one live without their mom, their best friend?* Her heart ached doubly due to her dad's death.

As happened on most of the other trips to and from seeing her mom, the song "Whom Shall I Fear? (God of Angel Armies)" by Chris Tomlin began playing on the radio. At that moment, she was struck with the realization that her mom missed her dad too. Soon her mother would be with her father and with her grandma and granddad too. The melody comforted her, soothing the pain in her heart. Tears streamed down her face as she drove across town to be close to her mom for a little while longer.

Jesus wants to comfort us in our sorrow. Sometimes he uses a song, a verse, or a quote. And often it takes place within our relationships. Difficult times can strengthen and deepen our bonds with our heavenly Father and loved ones if we allow him to work in our hearts. Jen discovered that in her most difficult season of life, God worked restoration and beauty in her family relationships. He can do that for you too.

—Beth

Music is the moonlight in the gloomy night of life.—
Johann Paul Friedrich Richter

PROMPT:

Is there a song, verse, quote, etc. that soothes your soul during difficult times? If so, write out the words below.

_____
_____
_____
_____
_____
_____
_____

Do you need healing in relationships? If so, how is God directing you to work on those relationships?

_____
_____
_____
_____
_____
_____
_____

CHAPTER 26

CRYING TOGETHER

Jesus wept. (John 11:35)

As a child, one of the best parts of Scripture memorization for me was learning the shortest verse in the Bible, "Jesus wept." As an adult, I think one of the most influential verses in the Bible is the same one: "Jesus wept."

Jesus had three special friends—siblings—whom he visited regularly. I picture Mary, Martha, and Lazarus as three single adults, living together. Their parents were gone. The Bible doesn't say why they lived together. Perhaps one was a widow. Maybe Lazarus was a bachelor. Perhaps their parents died before they could arrange marriages for all of them. But for whatever reason, these three lived together, and they were Jesus's close friends.

Then one day, Lazarus got sick. Mary and Martha called for Jesus because they believed he could heal their brother. But Jesus wasn't in a rush and took his time getting there. While he was still traveling, Lazarus died. As you can imagine, Mary and Martha were distraught. Jesus had healed other sick people. Why hadn't he come in time to heal Lazarus? He was their friend. Didn't he care?

When Jesus arrived four days after Lazarus had died, Martha ran to meet him, but Mary stayed at home. How sad Mary must have been. Was she angry, confused, or disappointed with Jesus? The Bible tells us that when Mary saw him, she fell at his feet and said, "Lord, if you had been here, my brother would not have died" (John 11:32).

Jesus saw her tears and was "deeply moved in spirit and troubled" (John 11:33). Mary and Martha showed him the tomb. This was when Jesus wept.

Imagine the emotions Mary and Martha must have experienced that day, devastated as they were by grief. Jesus showed them, with his own tears, how much he hurt too. Mary and Martha must have recognized his deep love. Picture the Son of God weeping along with your grief too. How comforting!

Jesus ordered people to remove the stone from in front of the tomb, and he called for Lazarus. Suddenly, Lazarus emerged from the tomb covered in cloth, looking like a mummy. Jesus ordered them to remove the bandages and give him clothes. Jesus performed a miracle that day. He did more than just heal a sick friend—he brought his friend back to life.

We rejoice in the miracle, but it is just as important to remember that Jesus wept. Jesus understood and experienced the same sorrow his friends encountered. And Jesus mourns with us. We don't walk through the valley of death alone. The Son of God walks with us. He understands our tears. Our hurts pierce his heart. God is with each of us in our hardest moments. He grieves along with us.

—Beth

O thou Omnipotent Good, thou carest for every one of us as if thou didst care for him only, and so for all as if they were but one! —Augustine

PROMPT:

Name your heartache. Picture Jesus's tears. Can you sense his arms around you, holding you, crying with you? Take a few minutes today to write and tell your heartache to Jesus. Remember that Jesus understands your pain.

_____

_____

_____

_____

_____

_____

_____

Read John 11:1–44 for the biblical telling of Lazarus's resurrection.

CHAPTER 27

A Voice in the Silence

Whether you turn to the right or to the left, your ears will hear a voice behind you, saying, "This is the way; walk in it." (Isaiah 30:21)

I was not in the habit of reading notes I found in the room of my teenage son, Ron. But when I spotted a piece of paper on his bed, a sinking feeling in the pit of my stomach compelled me to pick it up. It read, "I can't move across the country. I barely have any friends here, ones it took me forever to make. If my parents make me move, my life will be over. I'm scared I'll do something stupid and dark. Someone, please help me!"

My knees buckled. I crumpled to the floor, clutched the note to my heart and sobbed. Kevin ran into the room and knelt beside me. "Honey, what is it?"

With shaking hands, I unfolded the paper and handed it to Kev. "A suicide note from Ron," I said. "What are we going to do?"

Several weeks earlier, Kevin had accepted an offer to pastor a church over 2,500 miles from home. We'd already put our house on the market and were starting to pack. Kevin briefly scanned the paper, then shook his head. "This isn't a real suicide note, Jeanette. He doesn't want to move, so he's trying to play on your sympathy. He put that note on his bed in plain sight, so you'd find it."

I bolted upright, trading my sorrow for anger at my husband. How could Kevin not take this seriously?

Over the next few months, our opposite viewpoints created a chasm between us. Kev prayed that our house would sell so we could move. I prayed that God would protect Ron from hurting himself. And I hovered over Ron, telling him often how much we loved him.

The church called frequently to check on the status of our move. Kevin always had to tell them, "We're still working on it. Don't give up on us."

Several would-be buyers toured our house. A few seemed interested. But after six months, the now faded For Sale sign remained in the front yard.

Week after week, the distance between Kevin and me widened. Our once close and fun relationship had turned into a chore.

One morning as I paced in my bedroom, praying, I told the Lord, "This is an impossible situation. There is no solution."

That night Kevin and I decided to pray together after dinner to try to find specific directions from God. "We can't keep going on like this," Kev said.

We knelt beside our bed. I waited for Kevin to start praying. But he was silent. For five, ten, thirty minutes, we waited in a hushed, holy silence. I had no idea what Kevin was hearing from God. But my heart resonated with a sweet calm and the words, "Let it go." For the first time in months, I was able to put our marriage, our son, and our future into God's hands. I opened my eyes, looked over at Kevin, and raised my eyebrows. "What do you think?"

"We need to let this go, Jeanette. When the elders call, I will tell them that they'll need to find someone else to pastor their church." His voice was somber, but the worry lines between his eyes had disappeared.

Six years later, after Ron had graduated, God opened the door for us to move to Illinois—our happy place. Our marriage thrives once again.

I'm thankful God proved me wrong—there is no such thing as an impossibility with him—as long as we're willing to listen.

—Jeanette

> When one door of happiness closes, another opens. But often we look so long at the closed door that we do not see the one which has been opened for us.—Anonymous

Prompt:

Do you have a different viewpoint than someone you love? How has this caused a rift in your relationship?

_____

_____

_____

_____

_____

_____

_____

Spend some time in prayer, simply listening, with your loved one or alone. Write what God tells you:

_____

_____

_____

_____

YES, YOU CAN!

_____

_____

_____

_____

_____

_____

_____

_____

_____

_____

CHAPTER 28

FROM DEATH TO DANCING

"In the same way, let your light shine before others, that they may see your good deeds and glorify your Father in heaven." (Matthew 5:16)

After Jesus's death and resurrection, the brand-new church was given the Holy Spirit, and the good news began to spread. Peter, one of the twelve disciples, began traveling and preaching. One day he went to Joppa. This is where he met a disciple named Tabitha, or in Greek, Dorcas.

When we think of disciples, we usually think of men. But Luke, the author of the book of Acts, called this woman a disciple too. Everyone loved Dorcas. She was always doing good deeds, helping the poor, and making robes and other articles of clothing for all the widows in the town. One day Dorcas became sick and died. Friends washed her body and prepared it for burial.

Christians from Joppa ran to beg Peter to help. They guided him through an alleyway to the house where Dorcas's body lay. Her humble home was filled with half-completed sewing projects. Tunics lay in one corner. A threaded needle was still inserted in a robe. It was the workshop of an industrious woman.

Peter followed the women up the stairs to where Dorcas's body lay wrapped in burial garments. Widows gathered around her with tear-stained faces.

"Look at the stitching on this robe she made for me," said one woman as she pushed a delicately crafted garment into his hands.

"Here, look at mine." A second woman pressed forward.

It seemed they all had an article of clothing Dorcas had made.

The testimonials continued. "Dorcas helped me when my husband died. She brought me meals."

"She let me stay with her."

"She watched my children when my husband was sick."

"She noticed our needs. She saw us."

After hearing the stories of Dorcas's good deeds, Peter asked them to leave the room. Once alone, he said to the body, "Get up." Dorcas immediately opened her eyes and sat up. Peter took her by the hand and helped her stand. Then he called the believers, especially the women, back into the room.

Shocked and amazed, the women ran to hug their friend who was standing alive next to Peter. Soon the whole town heard of this miracle, and many believed in Jesus.

Throughout Dorcas's life, she showed Christ-like love to all in need. And through this early-church miracle, many put their faith in Jesus.

Dorcas showed that how we live matters. Our actions and good deeds point others to Christ, especially when hardships come, and we are still able to be a witness of his power in the world.

Today, we don't often see people brought back to life, but we do see lives transformed. For those who receive this miracle and those who witness it, it is a rebirth. Have you experienced the rebirth of salvation in your life? How is God using the new you to show the world his love?

Do you need a new life? Do you need a miracle? How can your life point others to Christ?

—Beth

Our deeds determine us, as much as we determine our deeds.—George Eliot

PROMPT:

How would you like God to use you? Will you be the tool God uses to lead others to him? What good deeds can you do? Who can you serve?

_____

_____

_____

_____

_____

_____

_____

Read Acts 9:36–42 for the biblical telling of Dorcas's story.

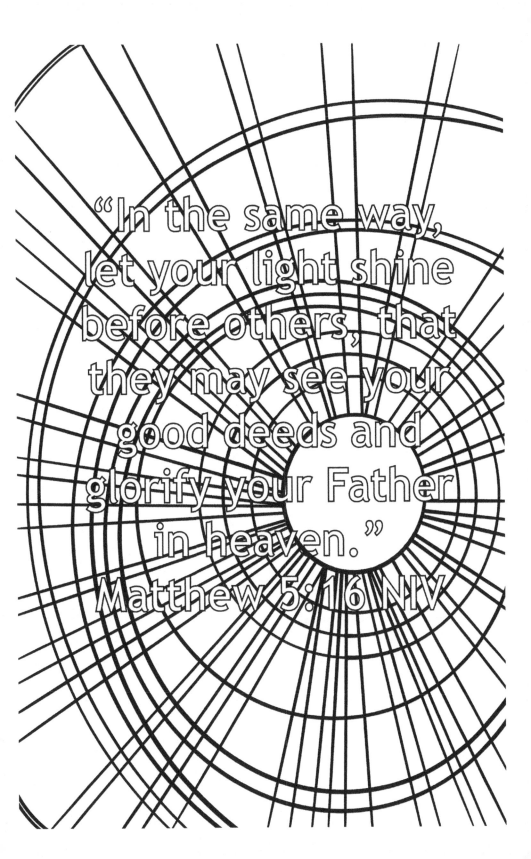

CHAPTER 29

SAVE MY CHILD, OR GIVE ME PEACE

The peace of God, which transcends all understanding,
will guard your hearts and your minds in Christ Jesus.
(Philippians 4:7)

"Ouch!" *Was that a contraction?*

I was only twenty-six weeks along with my third pregnancy. With every tightening of my abdominal muscles, my heart and lungs seemed to constrict also.

"No, God. This can't be happening. Not yet!"

Yet here I was, fighting off the fear and pain that were wrapping themselves around me like twin snakes.

We sat silently in the car, trying not to let our fears consume us as we drove the thirty minutes to the hospital. The doctor met us there and quickly barked out orders for a drug to stop labor and another to quicken the baby's lung development in case the labor couldn't be stopped.

A nurse wheeled me downstairs for a sonogram. "The baby is small, more like twenty-three weeks along. Do you want to find out the gender?"

That prompted the prayers for our tiny Jessica. *"God, she's too little for this world. I love her so, so much. Lord, help!"*

A few minutes later, my prayer turned into, *Lord, I believe you work miracles. I know you can save her. But more than anything, I want your will. I realize that if she dies before she is born, she will be with you. She will never experience pain. She will see only the beauty of heaven. And for Jessica, that would be the best life of all. You understand I want her. I want to see her little face, kiss her cheeks, and touch her toes. I want to watch her grow. I want to live the rest of my life in her presence. But if that isn't your will, I give her back to you. She's your creation. You love her more than I ever could. So, your will be done. It is well with my soul.*

Tears streamed down my face. My heart ached at what I had just prayed. *Had I just given God permission to take my baby?* Yet in that instant, I sensed an overwhelming peace. The Spirit whispered back, "All is well." God's love flowed deep in my soul. All would be okay. The path might not be easy, or what I wanted, but God was with me. I'll never understand how I was able to pray that prayer in my anguish and fear for the future. The only explanation I have is that God was working in my heat.

Several hours later, the contractions began to fade. My Jessie girl and I made it through the first battle. I went home to a life of strict bed rest … and no caffeine! Yikes!

Yet what a precious six weeks those were. My mom came to cook and clean, so my days were filled with prayers, healthy eating, and enjoying being pampered, along with permission to do what I loved with no guilt. I read all the books I could get my hands on, crocheted the largest afghan known to mankind, and made a cross-stitched blanket to honor my parents' fiftieth wedding anniversary.

A few weeks later, my due date came and went with no labor. The little stinker had decided she liked it in her warm, cozy home. So, after all the medicine I'd taken to stop the contractions, the doctor prescribed Pitocin to induce labor.

My new-found peace evaporated during delivery when I saw the doctor's face turn white. "Did you see that?" he asked Jeff, as the baby was quickly whisked away.

"What?" my mind began to whirl with worry.

"There's a knot in the umbilical cord," the doctor said as he followed her out of the delivery room.

I thought of my prayer of relinquishment months earlier. Did this mean God was going to take my baby after all? Panic threatened to overwhelm me, but then I remembered what the Lord had told me: "All is well." And indeed, God showed his kindness to me again when my baby girl was laid in my arms, screaming and healthy.

The doctor said, "She is a miracle!" He explained that her cord had had an actual knot in it. If it had pulled tight at any time during the pregnancy, she would have starved.

I thought back to the early labor. Was my body trying to end my pregnancy because of the knot? What miracles of protection had God done for us? What had he prevented as she moved, rolled, and kicked around inside me?

God is so compassionate. He helps in ways we can perceive, like giving us peace in the frightening moments. And then at other times he performs miracles we aren't cognizant of until much later.

—Beth

While you are proclaiming peace with your lips, be careful to have it even more fully in your heart.—Francis of Assisi

YES, YOU CAN!

PROMPT:

Where in your life are you longing for a miracle? How will you give your need to God?

_____

_____

_____

_____

_____

_____

_____

_____

_____

_____

_____

_____

_____

CHAPTER 30

JUST A TOUCH

Praise the Lord, my soul, and forget not all his benefits—
who forgives all your sins and heals all your diseases, who
redeems your life from the pit and crowns you with love
and compassion, who satisfies your desires with good
things so that your youth is renewed like the eagle's.
(Psalm 103:2–5)

As usual, a large crowd was following Jesus. Yet she
noticed this day seemed different. Jesus was passing by
"Anna's" house. She had been ill with a bleeding disorder—
and labeled unclean—for twelve years. She had heard the
stories of how Jesus healed the lepers. *If he could heal them,
surely he could heal me.* So Anna braved the crowd, weaving
in and out of people, pressing her way forward until she was
near the miracle-worker.

"If I can just get close enough, I'm sure to be healed." She
reached out, barely touching the hem of Jesus's robe. As soon
as her fingertips brushed the fabric, she recognized her pain
had dissipated.

"Who touched me?" Jesus stopped and turned around.

The crowd scoffed, not understanding why he would ask
such a question in the middle of the surging crowd. People
couldn't help but touch and bump into him constantly.

But the woman understood why he asked. "It was I."
Trembling, she approached her healer. "Teacher, I've been

sick for so many years, I'm not sure I even remember what it is like to be without pain. But I'd heard of your powers. When you passed by, I realized it was my chance. I thought if only I could get close enough to you, I might be healed. And the moment I touched just your robe my pain left."

He said to her, "Daughter, because you believed, you are healed. Go back home and live free from your suffering."

She left, praising God for the healing she'd experienced.

Some of us walk in physical, mental, or emotional pain for years. But God wants us to move toward him, to put one foot in front of the other, until we are close enough to touch him. All we need to do is reach out to Jesus. He will provide the healing. Sometimes it comes through doctors, therapists, or medication. Or we might find healing through answered prayer. For some, it comes through our promotion to heaven. But if we keep moving closer and closer to the healer, we will be restored.

—Beth

Although the world is full of suffering, it is also full of the overcoming of it.—Helen Keller

PROMPT:

Do you need to reach out to Jesus for healing? If so, ask God for guidance as you move closer to him. Write down the next step you will take. (Doctor, therapist, medication, prayer.)

_____

_____

_____

_____

_____

_____

_____

_____

_____

_____

_____

_____

Read Mark 5:24–34 and Luke 8:42–49 for the biblical account of the bleeding woman.

CHAPTER 31

THE FORGIVENESS FIX

He reached down from on high and took hold of me; he drew me out of deep waters. (Psalm 18:16)

Really, God? Is there no other way? Rita Dennis recoiled at the thought of bathing her elderly dad, Jim, who had been given only weeks to live. Rita's mom, Cathy, wasn't strong enough to lift her husband. And Rita's own husband, Dave, was away at work during the hours Jim was awake.

Rita took a deep breath, wiped away her tears, and started running the bath water. She recalled a time a few short years earlier when she'd had a conversation with her mom about end-of-life arrangements. "Mom, if Dad goes to heaven before you, I will gladly move you into my home and care for you. But if you pass away first, I will never take care of that dirty old man!"

Rita had reason for her revulsion. When she was fourteen and her mom worked night shift, her dad caught her alone in her room one night and touched her in ways that filled her with shame and disgust. A few weeks later, he exposed a private body part to her. Rita's former admiration and respect for her father turned to disappointment and revulsion. From then on, she made sure she was never alone with him. And she was afraid to tell her mom. She knew her mother had vowed that if Jim ever hurt Rita, she would kill him. *Then she must never find out!* Rita promised herself.

Four years later, during her freshman year of college, Rita shared with a close friend about her experience. "You have to forgive him," said the friend, "or you'll live with bitterness the rest of your life." The following week, Rita gathered her courage and visited her dad in his workshop behind their house. As she stepped through the door she prayed for the right words. "Dad, I came here to tell you that I forgive you for those two times when you … you know … you acted inappropriately toward me a few years ago."

Jim put down the birdhouse he was building, looked Rita in the eye, and stated, "That. Never. Happened."

Rita felt her face redden and her palms grow damp. *Now what? How can I forgive someone who refuses to admit he wronged me?* Rita sputtered a goodbye and drove back to her dorm room, her thoughts as dark as the night.

Over the next ten years, Rita married Dave, and they had their first child. Then, Jim received the diagnosis that his weak heart would soon give out. Knowing that Cathy also suffered from heart disease, Rita and Dave decided the only solution was to move both of Rita's parents into their home. Now, faced with the need to bathe her dad, Rita wondered if she and her husband had made the right choice.

"I know it's not a pleasant task," Cathy said, her gaze fixed on Rita. "But you'll just have to do it and get it over with."

If only she knew. Rita steeled herself for the ordeal.

After the bath, Jim sat on the edge of his bed in clean pajamas. His eyes and voice shone with a softness Rita had never seen before. "Thank you so much. I appreciate you doing this." Each time Rita did her father a favor, he thanked her. And each time that happened, her heart softened a little bit more toward him.

One night, Jim's sister—Rita's aunt—came to visit her dying brother. As they chatted, she mentioned her son doing something ornery. She turned to Jim. "But you've never been ornery, have you?"

Rita's dad held up two fingers and said, "Twice."

Rita breathed a sigh of relief. Her dad was finally admitting that he'd wronged her! In his backward way, he was asking her forgiveness. How could she refuse? A few short weeks later, when Rita said her final goodbye to Jim as he lay in his casket, her heart was free.

Of course, no child's trust should be trampled like Rita's was. There is no excuse for abuse. And, as unfair as it may seem, we don't always get the apology we deserve. Some people go to their graves never having righted the wrongs they inflicted on others. When we choose to forgive our perpetrators, like Rita did, despite their refusal to apologize, we open our hearts to unimaginable blessings. Because we're obeying Jesus's charge to release those who've wounded us, we're able to receive God's grace.

Do yourself a huge favor—forgive.

—Jeanette

Out of suffering have emerged the strongest souls; the most massive characters are seared with scars.—Kahlil Gibran

YES, YOU CAN!

PROMPT:

Have you had a hard time forgiving someone who wronged you?

_____

_____

_____

_____

_____

_____

Write a note to Jesus, thanking him for all the sins he's forgiven you for.

_____

_____

_____

_____

_____

Now, take some of the grace Jesus gave you when he chose to forgive you, and share it with the person who hurt you.

_____

_____

_____

_____

_____

CHAPTER 32

No Stones to Throw

You, Lord, are forgiving and good, abounding in love to all who call to you. (Psalm 86:5)

The crowd grew as people followed Jesus toward the temple where he usually taught. Excitement filled the air in anticipation of his next words. Suddenly a mob of men came barreling through the crowd, dragging a woman behind them, and throwing her at Jesus's feet.

The waif-like woman was a filthy mess. Wisps of disheveled hair blocked her view, tears and perspiration ran down her face, and her legs bled as a result of the cruel way she'd been dragged along the road.

"Teacher, this woman is an adulteress. The law says we must stone her. What do you say we do?" Disgust danced across the men's faces while treachery flashed from their eyes.

Jesus bent down and started writing in the dirt with his finger. The men kept pressing him for answers while Jesus took his time drawing letters and shapes in the dust and the woman lay trembling as she anticipated the first blow.

Jesus finally straightened and looked at the men with a piercing stare. "Whoever is sinless, let him be the first to throw a stone at her."

Slowly, one by one, the men walked away, heads down, recognizing they each had their own personal hidden sins.

Jesus reassuringly reached out to the confused woman. "Where are they? Has no one condemned you?'

"No one, sir," she said.

"Then I don't condemn you either," Jesus declared. "Now go and leave your life of sin."

Jesus must *be the one the people call the Messiah. Who else could save me from death?* Amazement and relief flooded through her. She was alive! But more than that, she was also forgiven. For the first time in her life, she experienced freedom from condemnation.

That day, the woman walked away from Jesus a different person. Everyone in the crowd recognized she had done wrong, yet Jesus chose to offer mercy instead of meting out the prescribed punishment.

This woman's story is a reminder of the importance of forgiveness. Have you ever been caught in your sin and labeled as deserving of punishment? If so, have you received grace instead of justice? Or are people's words and actions bruising you? Maybe you see your sin as unforgiveable. Remember that God still loves us even in our deepest struggles. He patiently waits to forgive us and to redeem our story. All we have to do is accept his forgiveness.

—Beth

I have always found that mercy bears richer fruits than strict justice.—Abraham Lincoln

PROMPT:

Have you ever done anything that caused others to condemn you—or at least you perceived they were condemning you? Can you accept Christ's forgiveness? Will you allow him to redeem you and use your past in a positive way? Name one step you can take toward accepting his forgiveness.

_____

_____

_____

_____

_____

_____

Read John 8:1–11 for the biblical account of the woman caught in adultery.

CHAPTER 33

Two Moms

He heals the brokenhearted and binds up their wounds.
(Psalm 147:3)

From the time Felicia was born, she and her mother, Emily, enjoyed a special bond. Emily had endured many miscarriages before Felicia came along, so she was thrilled to finally have a healthy baby to love. Felicia can still remember reaching between the slats of her crib for her mother's hand and her mother holding on until Felicia fell asleep.

As Felicia grew older, they took walks along the cornfield, by the chicken house, and through the woods where Emily would point out insects, birds, and wildflowers. Felicia grew up experiencing her mother's love.

But like most children, Felicia eventually left home. In college, she met Mark and fell in love. During Felicia's junior year, Emily became ill, so the couple decided to get married that summer. At the simple, sweet wedding, with only twenty-five in attendance, Felicia sensed her mom was tired. What she didn't realize was Emily was dying.

As Emily's sickness worsened, Felicia saw her mom as often as possible, each visit filled with lots of talking and tears. "The Lord is going to take care of you," Emily assured her. "You have a good man who will protect you and get you through this life without me. You have a good mother-in-law too."

Emily meant to assure her daughter, but her words had the opposite effect. As Felicia drove home, she sobbed, "I want *my* mom, not his mom." Tears blurred her view of the road ahead.

When Felicia's mother-in-law, Ada, found out about Emily's sickness, she reached out to her daughter-in-law. Although her kind words were what Felicia really needed, she wasn't ready to accept them. "You're not my mom. I want *my* mom," Felicia said, even though she recognized her response hurt her mother-in-law.

On a miserably hot August day, Emily died. In her deep grief, Felicia would sleepwalk, searching all over the house for her mother. Mark got up each time and guided Felicia back to the bedroom where he held her until she drifted off to sleep.

Several months later, Felicia was still fighting depression. Then one day, alone in her home, she sensed the presence of the Holy Spirit. "You will see your mom again," she heard him whisper to her heart. "It's time to let her go." A peace came over her, and for the first time since Emily's death, she was calm. God's peace gave her permission to start living again.

Eventually, Felicia got pregnant but lost the baby when she was just three months along. As soon as Ada heard the news, she came without even being asked and stayed with Felicia for a week, cooking, cleaning, and comforting. She did the same thing after the birth of every one of Felicia's three children and was also available whenever the couple needed a babysitter. Yet, Ada never pushed herself on them or interfered in their marriage. She set a beautiful example of how a wife, mom, and Christian woman should live her life.

Although Ada was an unassuming woman, she showed Felicia her love through her actions despite Felicia's harsh words years earlier. Ada taught Felicia how to love others unconditionally no matter what the circumstances might be or how the other person behaved.

Because Ada treated Felicia like one of her own, over time Felicia found it natural to call Ada "Mom," and Ada quietly filled the void left by Emily's absence. Ada even shared her favorite chocolate chip cookie recipe with Felicia. One day she tasted one of Felicia's cookies and asked, "Can I have your recipe?"

"Mom," Felicia said, laughing and rolling her eyes, "this is your recipe."

"Oh! These are just the best cookies I've ever had. They can't be my recipe." Ada winked at Felicia. And Felicia smiled, her heart warmed by the love of her second mom.

Felicia is grateful for the memory of her mother's hand comforting her, loving her, and guiding her throughout the years. She is also grateful for the gentle, loving presence of her mother-in-law, Ada, that has been a balm for her grieving heart.

When our hearts are broken and we struggle with empty places that loved ones used to fill, it can be difficult to allow others in. But those are the times when we especially need their love, kindness, and healing touch. Are you willing to allow others into your heart?

—Beth

All that I am or ever hope to be, I owe to my angel mother.—Abraham Lincoln

YES, YOU CAN!

PROMPT:

Has God filled a void in your life? Did you initially resist? Or are you resisting the healing God has for you? Write the name of someone or something you have lost on the line below.

_____

_____

_____

_____

_____

_____

Write the name of someone who you will allow to speak into your life and help you heal.

_____

_____

_____

_____

_____

_____

CHAPTER 34

SAY, WHAT?

My soul glorifies the Lord and my spirit rejoices in God my Savior (Luke 1:46–47)

"Joseph is so handsome, Mary! Aren't you excited to get married?"

Can't you just hear the giggling of Mary's friends as they chattered on about Joseph? Mary was grateful for being matched with someone so kind, gentle, and hardworking. She looked forward to life as the wife of Joseph.

Then one evening, everything changed. An angel appeared to her with the news she would have a child. Can you imagine her disbelief when being told she was pregnant without ever having been intimate with a man? Can you imagine the icy-cold fear that would have coursed through Mary's veins at what seemed to be an impossible situation?

Mary asked, "How can this be, since I am still a virgin?"

"The Holy Spirit will come upon you," the angel replied, "and the power of the Most High will overshadow you. So the holy one to be born will be called the Son of God ..." Then, as if perceiving how unbelievable his news must have been for her, he added, "For no word from God will ever fail" (Luke 1:37).

"I am the Lord's servant," Mary answered humbly, "May it be to me as you have said."

From that moment of obedience on, Mary's life was changed forever. For a while, it looked as if her fiancé, Joseph, would call off the wedding, but then an angel intervened. When it came time to give birth, she had to do so in the same room where animals were kept. Soon, shepherds came to worship the baby. Two years later, rich wise men arrived from a distant land and gave gifts of gold, myrrh, and frankincense to honor her toddler son. Soon after, an angel warned Mary and Joseph to flee to Egypt, saving their little son from certain death at the hands of a jealous ruler. When he was older, her son decided to stay behind after a temple visit, causing panic when his absence was discovered. As an adult, Jesus began doing miracles, and Mary was left in Nazareth to defend him against naysayers. Finally, she stood at the foot of a cross and watched her firstborn be put to death.

We can be sure this was not the life she had dreamed of living when she became engaged to Joseph. Her life turned out to be full of angel appearances, persecution from authorities, and heartache as her son became famous—even infamous—in some circles. But because of her willingness to obey, she has been honored down through generations, and the good news of her son's death and resurrection has been spread around the world.

If Mary can trust God with an unexpected pregnancy, death threats against her son, and then her son's crucifixion, we can certainly trust our trustworthy God with the unexpected situations we face. He sees the big picture.

- He knew that Mary would not be stoned to death as was the custom in those days for pregnancy outside of marriage.
- He knew Joseph would marry her, going against what culture expected him to do.

- He knew, well before Mary did, that her son was special because he was God's one and only Son.
- He knew all the miracles Jesus would perform, all the parables he would teach, and all the lives he would change.
- He knew of Jesus's death on the cross and his resurrection after three days.
- He knew that tiny baby inside Mary would become our sin-taker, our savior.

And God can use our situations for the good too. All we need to do is trust him.

—Beth

I avoid looking forward or backward, and try to keep looking upward.—Charlotte Bronte

PROMPT:

Are you facing a situation that seems impossible? When Mary faced that circumstance, she took time to sing a prayer of thanksgiving to God for his confidence in her. Read aloud her response in Luke 1:46–55.

Now take a few moments to write a response of your own, thanking God for choosing and enabling you to triumph in your situation.

_____

_____

_____

_____

_____

_____

_____

_____

_____

_____

_____

_____

_____

Read Matthew 1:18–25 for the biblical account of Mary's visit from the angel.

CHAPTER 35

I Don't Gotta Have It

My grace is sufficient for you. (2 Corinthians 12:9)

I gasped when I saw my credit card bill. It was three times higher than the previous month. "Do you think I'm addicted to spending?" I asked Kevin. My husband's gentle nature prevented him from agreeing with me. But I interpreted his silence as concurrence.

Over the years, I've learned that God knows more than I do. When I asked him the root cause of my penchant for overspending, he reminded me of a scene from my childhood.

During my sixth-grade year, I told Mom I needed some new school clothes. When she drove to Goodwill, I rushed from the car to the store, hoping none of my friends would see me. I knew Mom couldn't afford department store clothes. But having to wear clothes that had come from a thrift store made me want to crawl in a hole. I was afraid all 349 students at my junior high would know.

Laying the credit card bill aside to pay later that day, I got alone with Jesus in my prayer closet. "So I like to spend money to make up for not having enough as a kid," I said. It seemed to me I might be using the high I got from buying things, and the feeling of importance it gave me, as a drug. "But what can I do?" I wailed. "I can't simply quit spending money altogether."

Over the next few months, God showed me several practical ways to help myself crawl out of the pit of this spending addiction. The first way was to admit I had an addiction and couldn't free myself by my own devices. Just like an alcoholic or drug addict, I had to take that first brave step of acknowledging my powerlessness and asking the Lord for help. But it wasn't a once-and-you're-done thing. Every day, I still need to ask God to help me say no to my desire to fill up my emotional gas tank by buying things I don't need.

The second way I discovered that helps me stay strong is to spend time with my heavenly Father. The more I talk to him about every little thing in my life, no matter how insignificant it seems, the more I believe the high esteem he has for me. He gives me answers I couldn't find anywhere else. He fills me with confidence. His love makes me strong.

Finally, I chose a saying to keep me on track: "Live within your means." I have to get tough with myself. I often ask my husband for his input on purchases, using him as an accountability partner. Sometimes he says, "Go ahead and buy that pair of sandals—it's been a while since you had new shoes." Other times, his practical personality applies the brakes I need to not go into debt or purchase stuff merely for the sake of the high that spending gives me.

I won't lie and tell you that carrying out my decision to get free of this addiction has been easy. Almost like climbing the face of a cliff, it's sweaty, painful, even scary work. Denying myself means I have to trust God to fill my craving for significance. It's an inch-by-inch climb out of the pit of shame and debt.

What helps me most is the knowledge Jesus walks with me every step. He never condemns, never scolds, always cheers me on to victory. I feel his applause every time I overcome. Yes, I can. Because his grace is enough.

—Jeanette

Resolve not to be poor: whatever you have, spend less.—Samuel Johnson

Does at least one area of your life seem out of control?

If so, ask God to show you the reasons behind this hole in your heart.

_____

_____

_____

_____

_____

_____

What ways is he showing you to use to climb out of your pit?

_____

_____

_____

_____

_____

_____

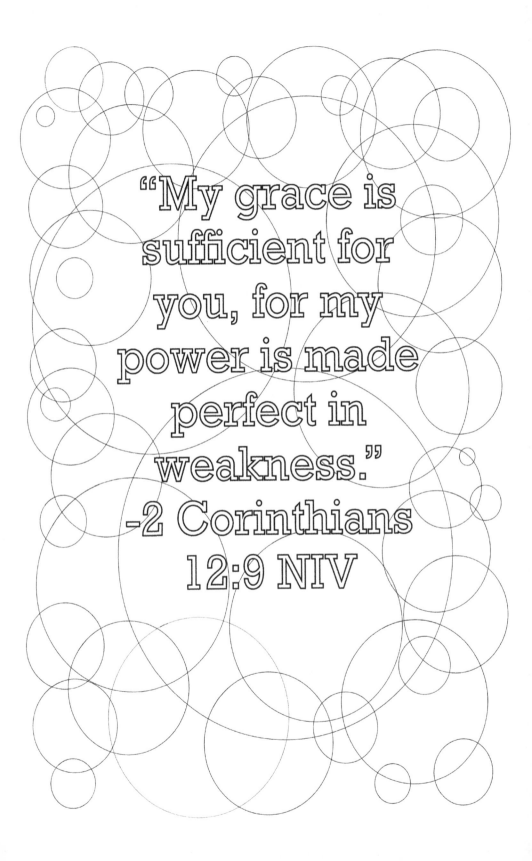

CHAPTER 36

THE FIRST EVANGELIST

I spread out my hands to you; I thirst for you like a parched land. (Psalm 143:6)

"Dinah" smiled to herself as she walked down the well-worn path to fetch water. She had looked forward to these few moments alone, away from town and away from other women's cruel words and judgmental glances. It was hard being the town outcast. Women looked at her as if she might steal their man, and their suspicions weren't without cause. She'd done that before.

But when Dinah reached the well, a foreign man was sitting beside it. *Just what I need. If anyone sees me at the well at the same time as a man, the rumors will fly.*

Fortunately for Dinah, this wasn't any ordinary man. He was Jesus, the Messiah, the Son of God. While he rested, the disciples had gone into town to buy food.

Dinah looked around guardedly before approaching Jesus.

As she lowered the jug off her head, Jesus watched her, then asked, "May I have a drink of water? I'm thirsty from my travels."

"Sir, why are you even talking to me? Don't you realize I'm a Samaritan?" *And worse than that, I'm the woman everyone in town avoids.* Dinah took a cautious step away from this strange man. *As if my reputation could get any worse.* She glanced quickly behind her to see who might witness this exchange, ready to gossip. Seeing no one, she asked, "Aren't you a Jew? How can you ask me for a drink? Why would you want to drink from the same jar as a Samaritan?"

"If you knew who you were talking to, you wouldn't ask me these questions," Jesus said. "You'd ask for living water instead." He grasped the jar offered, tilted his head back, and took a long, deep drink.

Dinah looked at Jesus in confusion. *He asked me for water, but then says I should ask him for water. How does he think can he get this living water with no jar of his own?*

Jesus smiled kindly. "Dinah, this water quenches thirst for a short time only, then you're thirsty again. The water I give is everlasting."

"Then give me that water so I won't have to keep coming to the well."

Jesus paused, searching her eyes. "Go, call your husband."

"Ha! I have no husband to call." Dinah's laugh was laced with bitterness.

"That's right. You've had five husbands. And the man you're with now isn't your husband."

"Who are you? A prophet?" Dinah looked at the ground, shuffling her feet. Jesus's penetrating gaze was too much for her.

He confused her even more when he said, "True worshipers will worship God in spirit and truth. God is spirit."

"I understand the Messiah is coming," she said, looking up again. "You Jews tell us that. But I don't understand what you are trying to say to me." Perplexed, she positioned herself to be ready to run.

"I am He, the Messiah."

Dinah had met the Living Water, Jesus.

She hurried and told the whole town about it. "Come. A man at the well knew all about me without my telling him anything. He is the Messiah!" Because of her report, many in Samaria believed in Jesus that day.

Some call Dinah the first evangelist. Meeting Jesus changed her life. Even though she was a woman of ill repute and the town outcast, she became the one to introduce her entire community to the Messiah.

Have you made wrong choices? Has your reputation been damaged? Take comfort in the fact that God wants to give you the living water. Your changed life can point others to Christ. Meeting the Savior changes us permanently, and others see the difference.

—Beth

The strongest principle of growth lies in human choice.—George Eliot

PROMPT

Do you need the living water? If so, pray this prayer today.

Jesus, you are the Messiah, the Living Water. Forgive me of my sins. Change me from the inside out. Amen

Write a prayer of thanksgiving to Jesus for being your Messiah.

_____

_____

_____

_____

_____

_____

_____

_____

_____

_____

_____

_____

_____

Read John 4:4–44 for the biblical account of the Samaritan woman at the well.

CHAPTER 37

A Foggy View

Give thanks to the Lord of lords:
His love endures forever.
to him who alone does great wonders,
His love endures forever.
who by his understanding made the heavens,
His love endures forever.
who spread out the earth upon the waters,
His love endures forever.
who made the great lights—
His love endures forever.
the sun to govern the day,
His love endures forever.
the moon and stars to govern the night;
His love endures forever.
(Psalm 136:3–9)

Bags were packed and the car was crammed full of everything the family was taking with them to Alaska. Thirteen-year-old Marlene hugged her older brothers and sister—Rich, John, and Ruth—wondering if she would ever see them again. It was time to say goodbye to certain family members, her beloved state of Wisconsin, and to lifelong friends.

Her dad had traveled to Anchorage to help build a church, and now he would become its pastor. While on his earlier trip, he had been captivated by the Alaskan wilderness, with its breathtaking mountains, glaciers, and churning rivers. Marlene's parents were excited for this midlife adventure. It was an adventure for Marlene, too, but also a time of sorrow. She was leaving behind nearly everything she'd known and loved. The road ahead may have been clear to her parents, but it was cloudy and a bit frightening for Marlene.

At the last minute, just as they were about to leave, Marlene couldn't find her glasses. She searched the car and her bag in desperation. As nearsighted as she was, she couldn't see much past her nose without correction. Not having her eyeglasses meant the 3,500 miles they'd be traveling through would be a blur to her. She wouldn't be able to share in the beauty of some of the most gorgeous scenery in North America.

Sadly, there wasn't time to wait for a new pair of glasses to be made—or even time for a trip to the eye doctor to get a prescription so glasses could be ordered immediately when they arrived in Anchorage. So, the family piled into the car and set off. Marlene stared out the backseat window, unable to see a thing. For days she traveled in a fog, grieving for what she'd left behind. Not just her glasses, but also her cousins, her friends, her home.

Each evening, the family of six stopped to camp. They tumbled out of the car, grateful to be out of its claustrophobic confines. Marlene felt the fresh air whispering on her face, breathed in the crisp aroma of pine trees, and heard the rustle of grass under her feet. She could see large objects well enough to help set up the canvas tent, make pine-needle paths around the campsite, and watch campfire flames leap and dance as she threw on bits of wood she'd collected. The best evening was when they camped right at the base of a beautiful mountain, its majesty looming in front of her.

Despite her nearsightedness, she could see the awesomeness of God's creation.

By the time the family reached Alaska, Marlene shared her family's excitement. She'd discovered Alaska's beauty included more than just epic vistas. She experienced Alaska through all her senses. And sharing that adventure with the ones she loved made up for her cloudy eyesight.

After they reached Anchorage, glasses were one of the family's first purchases. And soon, Marlene made a close-knit group of friends. Together they hiked and camped, enjoying all that the rugged landscape had to offer. On these adventures, Marlene's glasses helped her take in the beauty of her new home state. Alaska became her new home, and she ended up loving it just as much as she loved Wisconsin.

—**Beth**

> Happiness is a quality of the soul … not a function of one's material circumstances.—Aristotle

PROMPT:

Write about a situation you've gone through where you couldn't see clearly until you reached the other side. Take a few moments to thank God for his guiding, steadying hand.

_____

_____

_____

_____

_____

_____

_____

_____

_____

YES, YOU CAN!

_____

_____

_____

_____

_____

_____

_____

_____

_____

_____

_____

CHAPTER 38

WILL WE BE FORGOTTEN?

Lord, you have seen this; do not be silent. Do not be far from me, Lord. Awake, and rise to my defense! Contend for me, my God and Lord. (Psalm 35:22–23)

Outside Moses's tent, Milkah gathered her four sisters into a circle for moral support. "Now is the time. We need to stand together. Be strong. We can do this." As the five of them—Mahlah, Noah, Hoglah, Milkah, and Tirzah— grabbed hands and walked together, she added, "Remember. Let me do the talking."

After the daughters entered the tent where Moses sat settling disputes and their eyes adjusted to the dark interior, Milkah noticed many men standing around Moses, staring at them with judgmental looks. But the eyes of Moses were kind.

"Dear daughters, why are you here?" Compassion and warmth emanated from the wise old man.

The women hesitated, then Mahlah stepped forward.

"Our father, Zelophehad, had no sons. But he had the five of us daughters. Is it fair that our dear father's name should disappear, and our family be remembered no more? Please allow us to receive land like all the male leaders do. This is a fair request on behalf of our father, a descendent of Joseph."

Moses, Israel's leader, asked the Lord for an answer, and the Lord said to him, "What Zelophehad's daughters are saying is right. You must certainly give them property as an inheritance among their father's relatives and give their father's inheritance to them" (Numbers 27:6–7).

The decision was written down in the official record while the five women watched. "Oh, thank you, sir," Tirzah said. "Thank you for listening to our request and caring about our needs." Then the five sisters turned and rushed out into the sunlight. Laughing and hugging, they celebrated their good news together.

Isn't it good to see how our God values women? He is fair and just with us. Have you ever received unfair treatment as a woman or had to fight for your rights? Have you been abused, discriminated against, taken for granted, or belittled? Can you believe you are important to God? You are. God cares about the forgotten, the neglected, and the mistreated. God cares about you.

—Beth

We become brave by doing brave acts.—Aristotle

PROMPT:

Do you need to be brave? Do you need to fight for your case? Pray this Psalm to God today:

> "Lord, you have seen this; do not be silent. Do not be far from me, Lord. Awake, and rise to my defense! Contend for me, my God and Lord" (Psalm 35:22–23).

Read Numbers 27:1–11 for the biblical account of Zelophehad's daughters.

CHAPTER 39

A CHANGE OF HEART

Create in me a pure heart, O God, and renew a steadfast spirit within me. (Psalm 51:10)

I detested being a preacher's wife and having to deal with gripers who complained to me that my husband's beard was too long. I also disliked gossipers who spread rumors about us based on hearsay, and grumblers who were never satisfied no matter how hard we tried to accommodate them. I daydreamed of sitting in the pew each Sunday, a "normal" person. After I struggled through fifteen years of ministry, God granted me my desire.

When Kevin couldn't find a ministry position after leaving a successful youth ministry, he accepted a job at the office of a small business. Finally! I was free to be myself. At last, I wouldn't have to balance on anyone's rickety pedestal or be afraid to speak my mind. But then the truth slapped me in the face.

I soon realized whether I am wearing a hat labeled pastor's wife, homeschool mom, or office manager, people will judge me, criticize my family, and have unrealistic expectations, *simply because it's human nature to do so*. I couldn't run away from scrutiny and hurts by leaving leadership behind. I had just exchanged one set of challenges for another.

And Kevin was miserable.

He did an excellent job at the office. Over the course of ten years, he worked his way from bottom-rung office assistant to senior administrator. His boss regularly complimented him, saying what a pleasure it was to work with "a perfect gentleman." Nevertheless, Kevin's heart was not in balancing accounts and answering phones. He yearned instead to answer people's eternal questions and help them balance their lives by the power of God's Word.

Kev often shared with me his desire to develop more contentment—to be thankful for his job and enjoy his relationship with the Lord. I admired his mature attitude. But I also realized how much he longed to be back in the pulpit.

One morning as I prayed, the Holy Spirit convicted me of my attitude. He showed me that for Kevin to fulfill God's call on his life, I needed to be willing to relinquish my dream of not holding a leadership role. I wish I could tell you I immediately said, "Okay, God, I surrender all." Instead, it took several months before I was able to tell the Lord, "If my unwillingness to be a minister's wife is keeping Kev from getting another church, then I give up. I cannot stand to see him unhappy like this. If you want him to preach again, I'll not stand in your way. Your will be done, not mine."

No angel choirs appeared, singing, and dancing around the ceiling. No iridescent rose blossoms sprinkled from the sky. I didn't hear God's voice say, "Good girl. I am well pleased with you." I just knew he was, and that was enough for my heart to be at rest.

Several months later, we received a call to pastor a lovely Midwestern congregation, full of loving, generous folk. We've changed calendars twenty times since then, and we are still at that church, happier than ever.

God didn't make our lives trouble-free, persecution-free, and stress-free. But he's shown himself faithful in every trouble, persecution, and stressful situation. And he's given me the desire of my heart—to become a writer and speaker. The result? Wonder of wonders—a happy preacher's wife.

If God can change my heart from stone to pliable clay and even use me to change lives, he can move any mountain in your life. Yes, he can!

—Jeanette

Our greatest enemies, the ones we must fight most often, are within.—Thomas Paine

What situation in your life requires a change of heart?

_____

_____

_____

_____

_____

_____

If so, and even if you're not willing for God to change your heart, can you pray that he would make you willing?

_____

_____

_____

_____

_____

_____

What happy outcome can you envision as a result of your change of heart?

_____

YES, YOU CAN!

Create in me a pure heart, O God, and renew a steadfast spirit within me. -Psalms 51:1

CHAPTER 40

DOWN BY THE RIVERSIDE

But whoever looks intently into the perfect law that gives freedom, and continues in it—not forgetting what they have heard, but doing it—they will be blessed in what they do. (James 1:25)

In the heat of the afternoon sun, Lydia made her way out of the city, carrying a beautiful purple blanket—one of the purple textiles she sold that had helped her become wealthy. She smiled, thinking of the few moments of relaxation she would enjoy with other women gathered at the river. A ripple of laughter revealed where her friends sat. She dipped her feet in the shallow water, enjoying cool relief.

Several men approached and sat down near the women. "Have you heard the good news about Jesus of Nazareth?" one of them, Paul, said as he shared with the women about the birth of Jesus, the miracles he'd performed, teachings, and his death and resurrection.

Lydia already believed in the one true God and sensed a stirring in her heart. *Could this be true? Jesus is the long-awaited Messiah?* As Paul taught about Jesus being the Son of God, Lydia believed. In fact, her entire household believed and was baptized that day. Lydia's joyous conversion caused her to want to do something—anything—for God's kingdom. And as a woman of wealth and influence, she found ways to be useful to the spreading of the gospel and the beginning of the church.

Before Paul and the other men left that day, Lydia said, "I have a large home. You must spend your night there." They did so. Believers met there also. Not only did her house become the gathering place for Christians in Philippi, but Lydia also supported new Christians with her income as a dealer of purple cloth.

Lydia's life had been one of ease compared to those around her, but she did not yet have a relationship with Jesus. However, when she heard the good news, her heart responded. And after Lydia believed, God used her to bless others. He wants to use us too. Do you have something God can use? A home for a gathering? Money for someone's lunch? A car so you can take friends to church? A delicious pie to bless a new mom? A casserole for the grieving? A voice to speak up for the oppressed? A blog? A ministry?

When we know with God, our life purpose changes.

—Beth

Forever—is composed of Nows.—Emily Dickenson

PROMPT:

Are you ready to let God use you in new, exciting ways? How do you think God wants to work through you? Write out your thoughts and ideas in the lines below.

_____

_____

_____

_____

_____

_____

_____

_____

_____

_____

_____

_____

_____

Read Acts 16:13–15, 40 for the biblical account of Lydia.

ABOUT THE AUTHORS

BETH GORMONG

Beth Gormong is a writer, blogger, and fiber artist. When she's not writing her next book, knitting a sock, or planning in her Bullet Journal, you can find her hard at work at Trinity Lutheran Church. Beth loves the colors of nature, a little coffee with her creamer, and books on organization. She lives in a one-hundred-year old farmhouse in the middle of the country with her husband, Jeff, and two spoiled-rotten cats, Luna and Mo. She has three adult daughters who are off making the world a better place. Find her at www.bgormong.com or www. greengablestudio.blog.

JEANETTE LEVELLIE

Jeanette Levellie is an ordained minister, multi-published author, prolific speaker, and word addict. When she's not writing her next book, magazine story, or sermon, you can find her watching old movies with her husband or playing board games with her two kids and three grandkids. Jeanette loves bright colors, strong tea, and novels that help her forget her messy house. She also loves hearing from readers. Find her at www.jeanettelevellie.com.

Made in the USA
Columbia, SC
05 March 2021